TABLE OF CONTENTS

WELCOME TO TUNIS 9
Brief History and Overview of Tunis 9
Geography 11
Climate 12
Best Time to Visit Tunis 13
Essential Things to Pack for Your Trip to Tunis 15
Visa and Entry Requirements for Tunis, Tunisia 18

GETTING TO TUNIS 23
Getting to Tunis by Air 23
Getting to Tunis by Bus 28
Getting to Tunis by Train 33
Getting Around Tunis 38
Public Buses in Tunis 39
Metro Light Rail (Métro Léger) 43
Taxis in Tunis 48
Ride-Sharing Services in Tunis 50
Car Rentals in Tunis 53
Driving in Tunis 56
Walking Around Tunis 59

ACCOMMODATION OPTIONS IN TUNIS 63
    Luxury Hotels in Tunis..63

    Boutique Hotels in Tunis..68

    Mid-Range and Budget Hotels in Tunis....................72

    Hostels and Guesthouses in Tunis.............................78

    Riads in Tunis..83

TOP ATTRACTIONS IN TUNIS 95
    The Medina of Tunis 95

    Carthage Archaeological Site......................................98

    Sidi Bou Said...101

    The Bardo National Museum 104

    Zitouna Mosque..107

    Belvedere Park 109

    Cathedral of St. Vincent de Paul 112

    Habib Bourguiba Avenue..114

    Dar Ben Abdallah Museum.......................................117

    La Goulette 120

    Top Beaches in Tunis 123

OUTDOOR ACTIVITIES AND ADVENTURES IN TUNIS 131
    Hiking in Tunis..131

    Sailing in Tunis 133

Fishing Excursions in Tunis 135

Cycling Adventures in Tunis 138

Desert Excursions Near Tunis 143

DAY TRIPS AND EXCURSIONS FROM TUNIS 151

Dougga 151

Cap Bon Peninsula 153

El Jem 156

Zaghouan 159

Kairouan 161

DINING IN TUNIS 165

Must-Try Tunisian Dishes 165

Best Restaurants for Tunisian Cuisine 170

Street Food in Tunis 175

Cafés and Coffee Culture in Tunis 176

Vegetarian and Vegan Dining in Tunis 179

NIGHTLIFE AND ENTERTAINMENT IN TUNIS .. 185

Best Bars and Lounges in Tunis 185

Nightclubs and Live Music Venues in Tunis 189

Cultural Evening Experiences in Tunis 192

SHOPPING IN TUNIS 199
    Traditional Souks and Markets in Tunis 199
    Modern Shopping Malls and Retail Centers 204
    Tunisian Souvenirs to Take Home 210
    Shopping for Luxury Goods in Tunis.......................216

CULTURAL EXPERIENCES IN TUNIS 223
    Traditional Hammams 223
    Festivals and Events 228
    Religious Sites and Traditions in Tunis 234

PRACTICAL INFORMATION 243
    Internet and Connectivity 243
    Health and Safety 243
    Money Matters 244
    Local Language 245
    Emergency and Useful Phone Numbers...................245
    Local Laws 246
    Useful Websites and Resources 247

18 MUST-DO ACTIVITIES FOR A MEMORABLE EXPERIENCE IN TUNIS 251

SUGGESTED ITINERARY FOR EXPLORING TUNIS 255

CONCLUSION 259
PEN NOTES 261

"Allow your imagination to craft the scenes as you traverse through diverse and captivating landscapes different from your everyday horizon."

Michael Z. Wilson

WELCOME TO TUNIS

Nestled along the shimmering Mediterranean coast, Tunis is a city where ancient history intertwines with modern vitality. As the vibrant capital of Tunisia, this destination offers a rich blend of Arab, Berber, Ottoman, and French influences, creating a cultural blend that captivates every traveler. From its UNESCO-listed Medina to its bustling boulevards, Tunis invites you to explore its dynamic streets, historical treasures, and warm hospitality.

Brief History and Overview of Tunis

Tunis, the capital city of Tunisia, boasts a history that spans millennia. Its origins trace back to the Berbers, who established the area as an early settlement. However, it was the Carthaginians who first brought the region into prominence around the 9th century BCE. Located just a short distance from the ancient city of Carthage, Tunis served as a strategic hub for trade and military operations in the Mediterranean.

After the fall of Carthage to the Romans in 146 BCE, Tunis gradually grew in importance under Roman, Byzantine, and later Arab control. The 7th century marked a transformative period when the Arab Muslim conquest brought Islamic culture, architecture, and governance to the region. By the 12th century, Tunis had evolved into a flourishing city under the Hafsid dynasty, becoming a center for learning, commerce, and art.

During the Ottoman Empire, Tunis remained a significant regional power, blending its Arab-Islamic roots with Turkish influences.

The city later fell under French colonial rule in the late 19th century, leading to the development of its modern European-style districts. Tunisia gained independence in 1956, with Tunis as its vibrant capital.

Overview of the City

Today, Tunis is a dynamic metropolis that bridges the ancient and the modern. It is home to nearly 3 million people, making it the political, cultural, and economic heart of Tunisia. The city is divided into distinct areas, each offering a unique charm:

- **The Medina**: This UNESCO World Heritage Site is the historic core of Tunis, characterized by winding alleys, traditional souks, and iconic landmarks such as the Zitouna Mosque.
- **Ville Nouvelle (New Town)**: Developed during French colonial rule, this district features wide boulevards, European-style architecture, and modern amenities.
- **Carthage and Sidi Bou Said**: Located on the outskirts of Tunis, these areas showcase Tunisia's ancient ruins and picturesque coastal beauty.

Cultural Significance

Tunis is a cultural crossroads, reflecting influences from Berber, Arab, Ottoman, and French traditions. The city's museums, such as the renowned Bardo National Museum, showcase artifacts from Tunisia's rich past, including its Carthaginian, Roman, and Islamic heritage. Additionally, its vibrant art scene, traditional music, and festivals keep its cultural pulse alive.

A Thriving Urban Hub

In addition to its historical and cultural assets, Tunis is a thriving urban center with modern infrastructure, a growing economy, and a lively social scene. Visitors can enjoy everything from bustling markets and luxury shopping to fine dining and tranquil seaside escapes.

A Perfect Starting Point

Tunis serves as an excellent gateway for exploring Tunisia's diverse landscapes and heritage. Whether it's the ancient ruins of Carthage, the blue-and-white charm of Sidi Bou Said, or the golden sands of nearby beaches, the city is a perfect base for uncovering the country's many wonders.

From its rich past to its dynamic present, Tunis offers a journey through time and a glimpse into Tunisia's vibrant soul.

Geography

Tunis, the capital of Tunisia, is located in the northern part of the country, perched on the Mediterranean coast. The city lies along the Gulf of Tunis, a sheltered bay that opens into the Mediterranean Sea, providing a scenic coastal setting. Just a few kilometers northeast of Tunis are the ancient ruins of Carthage, adding historical significance to its geographical position.

The city is situated on a series of hills and plains, offering varied topography. To the east lies the Lake of Tunis, a shallow, brackish lagoon that connects the city to the Mediterranean via a navigable canal. This natural feature has historically contributed to the city's development as a key trade and transportation hub. Surrounding the city are fertile plains, which have supported agricultural activities for centuries.

Tunis serves as a central point connecting Tunisia's diverse landscapes, from the rolling hills and fertile farmland of the north to the arid expanses of the south. Its strategic location has made it a crossroads for commerce and culture throughout history.

Climate

Tunis enjoys a **Mediterranean climate**, characterized by hot, dry summers and mild, wet winters. This pleasant climate has made the city an attractive destination for travelers seeking both sun and culture.

- **Summer (June to August)**: Summers in Tunis are typically hot and dry, with average daytime temperatures ranging from 25°C to 35°C (77°F to 95°F). Coastal breezes from the Mediterranean help moderate the heat, especially in the evenings. Rainfall is scarce during this season.
- **Autumn (September to November)**: Autumn brings slightly cooler temperatures, ranging from 20°C to 30°C (68°F to 86°F), and occasional rainfall. This is an excellent time to visit, as the weather is comfortable, and the city is less crowded.
- **Winter (December to February)**: Winters are mild and wet, with temperatures averaging between 10°C and 16°C (50°F to 61°F). Rainfall is more frequent but rarely disruptive, and snow is almost unheard of in the city.
- **Spring (March to May)**: Spring offers mild, sunny days with temperatures between 15°C and 25°C (59°F to 77°F).

This is another ideal period for outdoor activities and sightseeing.

Best Time to Visit Tunis

Tunis is a year-round destination, but certain times of the year offer more favorable conditions for enjoying its rich history, cultural experiences, and outdoor attractions. The best time to visit Tunis generally depends on your preferences for weather, activities, and crowd levels.

Spring (March to May)

- **Why Visit?** Spring is one of the most delightful times to explore Tunis. The weather is mild and sunny, with temperatures ranging from 15°C to 25°C (59°F to 77°F). Flowers bloom across the city, adding vibrant colors to gardens and parks.
- **Activities**:
    - Wander through the Medina without the summer heat.
    - Explore the ruins of Carthage and other archaeological sites.
    - Enjoy outdoor cafes and terraces in places like Sidi Bou Said.
- **Crowds**: Moderate, making it an excellent time for peaceful sightseeing.

Summer (June to August)

- **Why Visit?** Summer is ideal for beach lovers and those seeking vibrant city energy. However, temperatures can soar between 25°C and 35°C (77°F to 95°F), with

occasional peaks higher inland. Coastal breezes help keep the city relatively comfortable.
- **Activities**:
    - Relax on nearby beaches or visit coastal resorts like La Marsa.
    - Experience festivals, such as the Carthage International Festival.
    - Enjoy Mediterranean evenings with cultural events and dining outdoors.
- **Crowds**: High, especially with international tourists and locals on holiday.

Autumn (September to November)

- **Why Visit?** Autumn brings cooler, comfortable temperatures ranging from 20°C to 30°C (68°F to 86°F). Occasional rains begin to appear, but they rarely disrupt outdoor plans.
- **Activities**:
    - Explore Tunis' historic landmarks and museums.
    - Visit local markets, where autumn harvests fill stalls with fresh produce.
    - Take day trips to nearby sites like Dougga or Hammamet.
- **Crowds**: Moderate to low, providing a relaxed atmosphere for exploration.

Winter (December to February)

- **Why Visit?** Winter in Tunis is mild, with temperatures averaging between 10°C and 16°C (50°F to 61°F). While

this is the rainy season, rain showers are usually short-lived and light.
- **Activities**:
    - Discover museums like the Bardo Museum without the tourist crowds.
    - Stroll through quieter souks in the Medina.
    - Enjoy traditional Tunisian dishes, especially warm stews and couscous.
- **Crowds**: Low, making it an ideal time for budget travelers and those seeking a tranquil experience.

Ideal Time Overall

- **Spring and Autumn** are considered the best times to visit Tunis. These seasons offer pleasant weather, manageable crowd levels, and opportunities to enjoy outdoor and cultural activities comfortably.

No matter when you choose to visit, Tunis offers a rich array of experiences, from its historic sites and cultural treasures to its coastal beauty and vibrant city life.

Essential Things to Pack for Your Trip to Tunis

Packing smartly for Tunis ensures a comfortable and hassle-free experience. The city's blend of history, culture, and Mediterranean charm calls for a mix of practical, weather-appropriate, and culturally considerate items.

Clothing and Footwear
- **Lightweight and Breathable Clothing**: Ideal for warm spring, summer, and autumn days. Cotton and linen fabrics are excellent for staying cool.

- **Layers for Cooler Evenings**: A light jacket or sweater is essential during cooler months (winter and early spring).
- **Modest Attire**: To respect local culture, especially when visiting religious sites, pack clothing that covers shoulders and knees, such as long skirts, loose trousers, and scarves.
- **Comfortable Walking Shoes**: The Medina's cobblestone streets and archaeological sites like Carthage require sturdy footwear. Sneakers or cushioned sandals are great choices.
- **Beachwear**: If visiting the coast, pack swimsuits, flip-flops, and a beach cover-up.

Travel Essentials

- **Passport and Visa**: Ensure your passport is valid and carry any required travel documents or visas.
- **Travel Insurance Documents**: A must for covering medical emergencies, cancellations, or unexpected events.
- **Copies of Important Documents**: Keep digital and paper copies of your passport, tickets, and accommodation confirmations.

Health and Personal Care Items

- **Sunscreen and Sunglasses**: Tunis' Mediterranean sun can be intense, so UV protection is essential.
- **Reusable Water Bottle**: Stay hydrated, especially during warm months. Consider a filtered bottle for added safety.
- **Basic First Aid Kit**: Include band-aids, pain relievers, anti-diarrhea medication, and motion sickness remedies.
- **Hand Sanitizer and Wet Wipes**: Useful for cleaning hands after navigating busy markets or public transport.

- **Toiletries**: Pack travel-sized essentials, as well as any prescription medications you may need.

Electronics and Accessories

- **Universal Travel Adapter**: Tunisia uses European-style plugs (Type C and E) with 220V.
- **Power Bank**: Useful for recharging devices on the go, especially when exploring the Medina.
- **Camera or Smartphone**: To capture Tunis' stunning architecture, historical landmarks, and scenic views.
- **Portable Wi-Fi or SIM Card**: For reliable internet access while navigating or staying connected.

Practical Items for Exploration

- **Guidebook or Map**: A physical guidebook or downloaded map can be handy for navigating areas with limited internet access.
- **Arabic Phrasebook**: Learning a few basic phrases, such as greetings, shows respect and enhances interactions.
- **Notebook or Travel Journal**: Perfect for jotting down memorable experiences or details about sites.
- **Daypack**: A small, lightweight backpack for carrying essentials like water, snacks, and sunscreen while sightseeing.

Seasonal-Specific Items

- **Rain Jacket or Umbrella** (Winter and Early Spring): Pack these for occasional showers during the rainy season.

- **Insect Repellent** (Summer): Helpful for outdoor activities during warmer months.

Souvenir Space

- Leave room in your luggage for souvenirs such as handwoven carpets, ceramics, or spices purchased from Tunis' bustling markets.

Visa and Entry Requirements for Tunis, Tunisia

Before traveling to Tunis, it is essential to check the visa and entry requirements specific to your nationality. Tunisia offers varying entry policies depending on the traveler's country of origin, the purpose of visit, and the intended duration of stay. Below is a detailed overview of what you need to know:

Visa-Free Entry

Tunisia offers visa-free access to travelers from many countries, primarily for short stays, usually up to 90 days.

- **Eligible Nationalities**: Citizens from countries such as most European Union (EU) nations, the United States, Canada, the United Kingdom, Australia, Japan, South Korea, and several Gulf Cooperation Council (GCC) states can enter without a visa for tourism or short-term visits.
- **Duration of Stay**:
    - Typically, stays are limited to 90 days within a 180-day period.
    - Some nationalities, such as citizens of Libya and Algeria, may benefit from additional privileges or longer stays based on bilateral agreements.

- **Passport Requirements**: Travelers must ensure their passports are valid for at least six months from their date of entry.

Visa Requirements

For travelers from countries not eligible for visa-free entry, obtaining a visa is mandatory.

- **Types of Visas**:
    - **Tourist Visa**: For leisure and tourism purposes.
    - **Business Visa**: For short-term business activities.
    - **Work or Study Visa**: For those planning to work, study, or reside in Tunisia.
- **How to Apply**:
    - Submit your application at the nearest Tunisian embassy or consulate.
    - Some nationalities may have access to an **e-Visa system**, allowing online applications for select visa categories.
- **Required Documents**:
    - Completed visa application form.
    - Passport-sized photographs.
    - Passport valid for at least six months.
    - Flight itinerary and proof of accommodation.
    - Proof of sufficient funds for the duration of stay.
    - Additional documents (e.g., invitation letter or proof of employment) may be required depending on the visa type.
- **Processing Time**: Processing times vary but generally range from 5 to 15 business days.

Special Entry Conditions

- **Transit Without Visa (TWOV)**: Travelers transiting through Tunis-Carthage International Airport for less than 24 hours may not need a visa, provided they remain in the airport's transit area.
- **Group Travel Exemptions**: Organized tourist groups from certain countries may be allowed entry without individual visas if the trip is arranged through a recognized tour operator.
- **Diplomatic and Official Passports**: Holders of diplomatic or official passports from many countries may be exempt from visa requirements for official visits.

Arrival Requirements

Regardless of visa status, travelers must meet the following requirements upon arrival:

- **Health and Vaccination**:
    - Proof of yellow fever vaccination may be required if you are arriving from a country with a yellow fever risk.
    - COVID-19 regulations (if applicable) may include vaccination certificates or negative test results; check for the latest updates.
- **Proof of Return or Onward Travel**: Airlines and immigration authorities may require evidence of return or onward tickets.
- **Proof of Funds**: Immigration officers may ask for proof that you have sufficient funds to cover your stay.

Extensions and Overstay

- **Extensions**: Visitors needing to stay beyond their permitted period must apply for an extension through the Tunisian Ministry of Interior or local immigration offices before their authorized stay expires.
- **Penalties for Overstaying**: Overstaying your visa-free or visa-permitted duration may result in fines, detention, or deportation.

Helpful Tips for Travelers

- **Check Requirements in Advance**: Entry requirements can change, so always confirm with a Tunisian embassy or consulate before your trip.
- **Travel Insurance**: While not always mandatory, comprehensive travel insurance covering medical emergencies, trip cancellations, and other potential issues is strongly recommended.
- **Stay Updated**: Monitor Tunisia's official immigration or government travel websites for the latest entry rules, especially for health-related regulations.

GETTING TO TUNIS

Tunis, the vibrant capital of Tunisia, is an exciting gateway to North Africa, offering a unique blend of ancient history, rich culture, and modern attractions. To ensure your journey to Tunis is seamless and enjoyable, here's a comprehensive guide to getting to the city, with essential tips for travelers.

Getting to Tunis by Air

Tunis, the vibrant capital of Tunisia, is a bustling city that attracts tourists from around the world, thanks to its rich history, culture, and modern amenities. Traveling to Tunis by air is the most common and convenient method for international travelers. Here's a comprehensive guide on how to get to Tunis by air, including important tips and information to make your journey as smooth as possible.

Tunis-Carthage International Airport (TUN)

The main international gateway to Tunis is **Tunis-Carthage International Airport (IATA: TUN)**, located approximately 8 kilometers northeast of the city center. This airport is the busiest in Tunisia and serves as a hub for **Tunisair**, the country's national airline, as well as several international carriers.

- **Airport Facilities**: Tunis-Carthage International Airport offers a range of services for travelers, including currency exchange, ATMs, duty-free shops, restaurants, lounges, and free Wi-Fi. There are also car rental services available at

the airport, which is convenient for those wishing to explore the city and beyond independently.
- **Terminal Information**: The airport has one main terminal serving both international and domestic flights. It is modern, well-signposted, and equipped with basic amenities to ensure a comfortable experience for passengers.

International Flights to Tunis

Tunis-Carthage International Airport is well-connected to major cities around the world, making it easy for travelers to reach the city by air. The airport handles numerous flights from Europe, the Middle East, and Africa, with direct and connecting routes available.

- **Major Airlines Operating to Tunis**:
    - **Tunisair**: As the national carrier, **Tunisair** offers frequent flights from major cities like Paris, London, Istanbul, and Dubai.
    - **European Airlines**: Popular European airlines like **Air France**, **Lufthansa**, **Ryanair**, **Alitalia**, and **British Airways** provide direct flights to Tunis from cities such as **Paris**, **Rome**, **Frankfurt**, **London**, and **Madrid**.
    - **Middle Eastern Airlines**: Airlines like **Qatar Airways**, **Emirates**, and **Turkish Airlines** offer convenient connections between Tunis and major cities in the Middle East, including Doha, Dubai, and Istanbul.

- ○ **African Airlines**: Regional flights are available from cities in neighboring countries, such as **Algiers**, **Tripoli**, and **Cairo**.
- **Direct and Connecting Flights**: Depending on your departure city, you can opt for direct flights to Tunis or connect via major international hubs. Direct flights are generally faster but may be more expensive. Connecting flights can offer more flexibility and potentially lower fares, although they may take longer.

Booking Your Flight to Tunis

When booking a flight to Tunis, keep the following tips in mind:

- **Book in Advance**: To get the best deals on flights, it's advisable to book your tickets several weeks or even months in advance, especially during peak travel seasons (such as summer and major holidays).
- **Flight Comparison Websites**: Use online flight comparison websites like **Skyscanner**, **Google Flights**, or **Kayak** to compare prices across multiple airlines and booking platforms.
- **Travel Seasons**: The best time to visit Tunis is generally between **April and June** or **September and November**, when the weather is pleasant and the tourist crowds are more manageable. Flights during the summer months (July and August) can be more expensive due to the peak tourist season.
- **Flexible Dates**: If you have flexibility in your travel dates, you may find cheaper flight options. Mid-week flights (Tuesday and Wednesday) are often less expensive than weekend flights.

Arrival at Tunis-Carthage International Airport

Once you arrive at Tunis-Carthage International Airport, you'll need to navigate the airport's arrival procedures and transportation options.

- **Immigration and Customs**: Upon arrival, travelers will pass through immigration control, where you may be asked to show your passport, visa (if required), and flight details. Tunisia is a member of the **Schengen Area**, so citizens from Schengen member countries generally don't require a visa for short stays (up to 90 days). Travelers from other countries may need to check visa requirements ahead of time.
- **Baggage Claim**: After clearing immigration, proceed to the baggage claim area to collect your luggage. The airport is relatively small, so it should be easy to find your luggage belt.
- **Customs Declaration**: Tunisia enforces customs regulations that limit the amount of duty-free goods you can bring into the country. Be sure to familiarize yourself with the limits to avoid any issues at customs. If you're carrying any restricted items (such as large amounts of currency or certain electronics), you may need to declare them.

Transportation Options from Tunis-Carthage Airport to the City Center

Once you've cleared immigration and collected your luggage, you'll need to get from the airport to your accommodation in the city center. Here are the most common options:

- **Taxis**: Taxis are readily available outside the airport terminal. A taxi ride to central Tunis takes approximately 15 to 20 minutes, depending on traffic. It's a good idea to agree on a fare before you depart, though most taxis will use a meter. A typical fare ranges from 15 to 25 Tunisian Dinars (TND). Make sure you have cash in Tunisian Dinars (TND) as many taxis don't accept credit cards.
- **Airport Shuttle**: There are shuttle buses that operate between the airport and downtown Tunis, as well as major tourist locations. These shuttles are generally more affordable than taxis, but they may take longer due to multiple stops. Tickets can be purchased at the airport's transportation desk.
- **Private Transfers**: For a more comfortable, hassle-free experience, many travelers opt to book private airport transfers in advance. This option allows for door-to-door service and is ideal for those carrying heavy luggage or traveling in a group. Private transfer services can be booked online through various travel agencies or directly with local service providers.
- **Car Rentals**: If you plan on exploring beyond Tunis or prefer the flexibility of having your own vehicle, you can rent a car at the airport. Major international car rental agencies, such as Europcar, Hertz, and Avis, have desks at Tunis-Carthage International Airport. Ensure that you have an international driving permit (IDP) if required, and familiarize yourself with local driving laws.

Tips for Smooth Air Travel to Tunis

- **Flight Delays and Cancellations**: Be prepared for potential delays, especially during the busy summer months. It's advisable to confirm your flight status before heading to the airport, and always allow for extra time when making connections. If your flight is delayed, check with the airline about compensation or rebooking options.
- **Luggage Restrictions**: Be aware of the baggage policies of your airline, especially if you're flying with a budget carrier. Many airlines impose stricter baggage weight limits or charge additional fees for checked baggage. Always check the baggage allowance before packing.
- **Language**: Arabic is the official language of Tunisia, but French is widely spoken, especially in urban areas and at the airport. English is also understood at the airport, particularly in the main tourist areas. Knowing basic French or Arabic phrases can be helpful when navigating the airport and other travel-related situations.
- **Arrival Time**: Arrive at least **3 hours prior to your international flight** and **2 hours for domestic flights** to allow enough time for check-in, security screening, and potential delays.

Getting to Tunis by Bus

Traveling to Tunis by bus is an affordable and convenient option for those wishing to explore Tunisia and its surroundings. The bus network in Tunisia is extensive and connects Tunis with other cities, towns, and regions. Whether you're coming from nearby cities within Tunisia or neighboring countries, here's a comprehensive guide to traveling to Tunis by bus, including essential tips and information.

Overview of Bus Travel to Tunis

Tunis is well-served by both domestic and international bus routes, making it an easy destination to reach by land. Whether you're coming from other cities in Tunisia or traveling across borders, buses provide a reliable and cost-effective means of transport. The bus stations in Tunis are centrally located and well-connected to public transport networks, offering easy access to the city center.

- **Main Bus Stations in Tunis**:
    - **Gare Routière de Tunis (Tunis Central Bus Station)**: This is the main bus station in Tunis, located in the heart of the city. It is the central hub for intercity and regional buses arriving from within Tunisia.
    - **Tunis Port Bus Station**: Located near the port, this station handles buses arriving from various destinations, including ferries coming from Italy and Malta.
    - **Tunis-Carthage Airport**: For travelers arriving by plane, some buses provide services directly from the airport to the city center, as well as to key destinations in Tunis.

Domestic Bus Routes to Tunis

Tunis is the primary hub for bus routes connecting the capital to other cities and regions within Tunisia. Buses provide a convenient and affordable way to travel between Tunis and popular destinations across the country.

- **Tunis to Major Cities in Tunisia**:
    - **From Sousse**: The bus ride from Sousse to Tunis takes around **2 hours** and runs frequently throughout the day. Sousse is a popular coastal town, and there are both private and public buses operating this route.
    - **From Hammamet**: Buses between Hammamet and Tunis are available and take around **1.5 to 2 hours**, with frequent services throughout the day.
    - **From Sfax**: Travel from Sfax to Tunis takes around **4 to 5 hours** by bus, depending on the route. Buses are generally direct, though some may stop in smaller towns along the way.
    - **From Kairouan**: This city, rich in history, is about **3 hours** from Tunis by bus. There are several buses operating daily between Kairouan and Tunis.
    - **From Tozeur**: Buses from the southern town of Tozeur to Tunis typically take around **7 hours**, with limited services during the day. It's advisable to check schedules in advance for longer journeys like this one.
- **Bus Companies**: The main bus operators within Tunisia include **SNT** (Société Nationale des Transports), the national bus company, and private companies such as CTN (Compagnie Tunisienne de Navigation), Karama Travel, and Tunis Travel. Buses operated by SNT are generally

more affordable, while private companies may offer more comfort and speed.
- **Bus Types**: Buses in Tunisia range from basic, local service buses to more comfortable long-distance coaches. Long-distance buses typically have air conditioning, more spacious seating, and sometimes onboard snacks. Ensure you check the comfort level and amenities of your bus before booking.

International Bus Routes to Tunis

Tunis is also easily accessible by bus from several neighboring countries, making it an excellent destination for travelers coming from Algeria, Libya, and even Malta. International bus travel can be an affordable and scenic way to reach the capital.

- **From Algeria**: Bus services run from Algiers to Tunis, with the journey taking approximately 6 to 7 hours. Buses depart from various locations in Algiers, including the central bus station. Most buses are operated by private companies, and it's recommended to book in advance, especially during busy seasons.
- **From Libya**: There are also buses from Tripoli, Libya, to Tunis, although these services are less frequent. The journey typically takes around 6 to 7 hours, and the buses are operated by both local and international companies. Travelers should check current travel advisories and border crossing requirements before booking tickets.
- **From Malta**: Traveling by bus from Malta to Tunis is possible by taking a ferry from Malta's port to Tunis, followed by a bus ride into the city. Ferries run regularly, and buses from the port connect to downtown Tunis. The

combined ferry and bus journey usually takes around 8 to 10 hours.
- **From Egypt**: Though less common, buses are available from Cairo to Tunis, with the journey taking around 10 to 12 hours. Be sure to check bus schedules and book tickets in advance as this route can have fewer departures.
- **Bus Travel Comfort**: International buses tend to offer a higher level of comfort, with amenities such as Wi-Fi, air-conditioning, and reclining seats. However, the journey may be longer and less predictable due to border crossings and customs checks, so it's essential to plan accordingly.

Booking Bus Tickets

Tickets for buses to and from Tunis can be purchased in various ways:

- **Online Booking**: Many bus companies, especially those operating on longer routes, allow passengers to book tickets online through their official websites or through third-party booking platforms. This is the most convenient option for reserving seats in advance, especially during peak travel seasons.
- **At the Bus Station**: You can also purchase tickets directly at the bus station, either from the ticket counters or from agents located near the bus platforms. However, this option can be time-consuming, and tickets may sell out during busy periods.
- **Travel Agencies**: If you're unsure about bus schedules or prefer assistance, travel agencies in Tunisia often provide bus booking services for both domestic and international routes. This can be a helpful option for first-time visitors.

- **Pricing**: Bus tickets in Tunisia are generally very affordable compared to other forms of transportation. Prices vary depending on the distance, bus company, and the level of comfort. For example, a bus ticket from Sousse to Tunis can cost around **10 to 20 TND** (Tunisian Dinars), while a longer trip, such as from Sfax to Tunis, may cost between **20 and 30 TND**.

Tips for Bus Travel to Tunis

- **Travel During Off-Peak Hours**: To avoid overcrowded buses and potential delays, try to travel during off-peak hours. Buses can be especially busy during school holidays, summer months, and religious festivals, so booking your ticket in advance is advisable.
- **Arrive Early**: Arriving at the bus station at least 30 minutes before departure is recommended, as this gives you enough time to find your bus, get settled, and avoid any last-minute rush.
- **Carry Essentials**: While Tunisian buses typically stop for breaks on longer routes, it's a good idea to bring water, snacks, and a small bag for personal essentials to make the journey more comfortable.
- **Keep Your Documents Handy**: On international routes, customs and border checks may require you to present identification and other documents. Ensure you have your passport, visa (if necessary), and bus ticket readily available.
- **Stay Safe**: As with all bus travel, ensure your valuables are securely stored, and always be aware of your surroundings. Although Tunisia is generally a safe country, it's always prudent to take basic safety precautions.

Getting to Tunis by Train

Tunis, the bustling capital of Tunisia, is well-connected by train to many cities across the country, offering travelers a comfortable and scenic way to explore the region. Train travel is one of the most popular and efficient forms of transportation within Tunisia, and it provides an excellent opportunity to experience the country's landscapes and culture. Here's a comprehensive guide to getting to Tunis by train, including essential tips and information for travelers.

Overview of the Tunisian Rail Network

Tunisia boasts a well-developed railway system that connects major cities, towns, and regions. The **Société Nationale des Chemins de Fer Tunisiens (SNCFT)**, the national railway company, operates most of the train services in Tunisia. Trains are reliable, affordable, and an excellent way to travel between Tunis and other destinations across the country.

- **Train Stations in Tunis**:
    - **Gare de Tunis (Tunis Central Railway Station)**: Located in the city center, this is the main station for domestic and international train services. It is a hub for most regional and intercity trains, making it the primary station for travelers arriving by train.
    - **Gare de la Goulette**: This station is located near the port area and serves trains that connect to the coastal areas and towns. It's a good station for travelers heading to the northern suburbs or the port of Tunis.

- **Types of Trains**: Tunisia offers different types of trains depending on the route and level of comfort. The most common services are:
    - **Luxe Trains**: These are more comfortable trains, often with air-conditioned compartments, that operate on longer routes.
    - **Ordinary Trains**: These are standard trains that connect smaller towns and cities. They may not have the same level of comfort but are still a reliable and affordable option for travelers.

Domestic Train Routes to Tunis

Tunis is a key destination on the Tunisian railway network, with frequent train services to and from various cities. Whether you are coming from the coastal regions, inland cities, or towns in the south, taking a train to Tunis offers a comfortable and scenic travel experience.

- **From Major Cities in Tunisia**:
    - **From Sousse**: Trains BB the day, and the route offers beautiful views of the Mediterranean coastline.
    - **From Hammamet**: A train ride from Hammamet to Tunis takes about 1.5 to 2 hours, with trains operating every 1 to 2 hours. The trains are generally comfortable and provide air-conditioned carriages.
    - **From Sfax**: The train journey from Sfax to Tunis is around 4 to 5 hours, and trains depart several times per day. This route is serviced by both standard and

> higher-class trains, with the option of air-conditioned carriages.
>   - **From Kairouan**: Kairouan is around 3 hours from Tunis by train. The route provides travelers with a comfortable and scenic journey through the Tunisian countryside.
>   - **From Gabès**: For those traveling from the southern regions of Tunisia, trains from Gabès to Tunis take approximately 7 hours. These longer routes may involve transfers at larger stations like Sfax.
> - **Train Schedules**: Train services to and from Tunis are generally regular, but the frequency may decrease during public holidays or off-peak seasons. It's a good idea to check schedules ahead of time, especially for longer journeys. You can check train schedules and availability on the **SNCFT** website or visit the train station.

International Train Routes to Tunis

Tunis is also accessible by train from neighboring countries, making it a great destination for international travelers coming from Algeria or Libya. The international rail services are less frequent than domestic ones, but they offer a convenient and affordable option for those wishing to travel by train.

- **From Algeria**: There are occasional trains from Algiers to Tunis, although the service is not as frequent as domestic routes. The journey can take 6 to 7 hours, and travelers should check schedules in advance, as services can be limited.
- **From Libya**: International train services from Tripoli to Tunis are available, though they are less common. This

route can take around 6 to 7 hours, and travelers should verify schedules due to occasional changes or disruptions in service.
- **From Tunisia to Malta**: While there are no direct train services between Tunisia and Malta, travelers can take a ferry from Tunis to the island of Malta and then continue their journey by train once in Europe.

Booking Train Tickets to Tunis

There are several ways to purchase train tickets for travel to and from Tunis, offering flexibility for travelers. Here are your options:

- **Online Booking**: SNCFT offers online booking for many of their routes. Tickets can be purchased through their official website or via third-party platforms. This is the most convenient way to ensure a reserved seat, especially for long-distance or intercity travel.
- **At the Train Station**: Tickets for trains to Tunis can be purchased at the train stations, either from ticket counters or automated ticket machines. For popular routes, it's advisable to arrive early to secure a ticket, particularly during peak travel times.
- **Travel Agencies**: Some travel agencies in Tunisia also offer train ticket booking services. This can be a helpful option for tourists who prefer assistance or wish to arrange their travel plans with the support of a local agent.
- **Pricing**: Train tickets in Tunisia are generally very affordable, with prices depending on the distance and train class. For example:
    - A ticket from Sousse to Tunis might cost **10-20 TND**.
    - A longer journey, such as from Sfax to Tunis, may cost between **20 and 30 TND**.
    - International routes tend to be slightly more expensive, with tickets from Algeria or Libya costing around 30-50 TND depending on the route.

Tips for Traveling by Train to Tunis

- **Arrive Early**: It's advisable to arrive at the train station at least 30 minutes before departure to allow for ticket purchase, baggage handling, and finding your platform. Trains can be busy during peak hours, so early arrival ensures you get the best seats.
- **Check the Schedule**: While trains are generally punctual, delays can occasionally occur, especially during high traffic times or bad weather. Always check the departure boards at the station for any updates on train schedules.
- **Language**: The primary language in Tunisia is Arabic, though French is widely spoken, especially at train stations. Most train staff will understand basic English, but it's helpful to know a few phrases in French or Arabic to make your travel smoother.
- **Keep Your Ticket Safe**: During the journey, ticket inspectors may come through the train to check your ticket. Make sure you keep it handy and secure to avoid any problems. You may also need to show identification if traveling on international routes.
- **Travel Light**: Although Tunisia's trains are generally comfortable, space for luggage can be limited, especially on busy trains. Keep your luggage compact and easy to manage, and be mindful of space in overhead racks or luggage compartments.

Getting Around Tunis

Navigating Tunis, the vibrant capital of Tunisia, is an adventure in itself. From the bustling medina to the tranquil suburbs, a variety of transportation options makes exploring this historic city both convenient and affordable. Here's a detailed guide to help travelers get around Tunis with ease.

Public Buses in Tunis

Tunis offers a diverse and affordable public transportation network, with buses being one of the most commonly used options for getting around the city and its surrounding areas. Operated by the Société des Transports de Tunis (TRANSTU), the bus system is reliable, accessible, and an ideal choice for travelers seeking to experience the local rhythm of the city.

Overview of the Bus System

The bus system in Tunis is extensive, covering the city's central neighborhoods, residential suburbs, and even nearby towns. There are over 100 bus routes in operation, and they provide an excellent means of travel for both tourists and locals. The buses are modern, comfortable, and equipped with air conditioning, especially on longer routes.

- **Types of Buses:**
    - **City Buses:** These buses are primarily used for traveling within Tunis itself, including major areas like the Medina, the airport, and other urban districts.
    - **Suburban Buses:** These buses connect Tunis with suburban neighborhoods and towns like La Marsa, Carthage, and Ariana.
    - **Intercity Buses:** Buses that extend beyond the capital, linking Tunis to other cities across Tunisia,

including places like Sousse, Kairouan, and Monastir.

Bus Routes and Timetables

- **Route Information:**
    - Bus routes in Tunis are clearly marked with numbers and destinations displayed on the front and side of the buses. Major terminals, like Bab el Bhar (Porte de France) or the main bus station at Tunis Marine, serve as starting points for most of the routes.
    - Most bus routes operate from early morning until late evening, with some buses running 24/7 for areas like the airport or central locations.
    - During peak hours, buses can get crowded, especially those traveling to and from the city center, so it's advisable to plan your trip accordingly.
- **Timetables:**
    - Bus schedules can vary by route, with major lines running frequently during the day (every 10 to 15 minutes), while less busy routes may operate with longer intervals.
    - For more accurate timetable details, it's best to check local timetables posted at bus stations or ask for assistance at major stops.

Ticketing System and Fares

- **Ticket Prices:**

- Bus fares are quite affordable, with a single ride typically costing around 0.5 to 1 Tunisian dinar (TND), depending on the distance traveled. Long-distance routes to suburban areas may have slightly higher fares.
  - You can purchase tickets directly from the bus driver or at ticket kiosks located at major bus stations. It's advisable to carry small change, as some drivers may not have enough change for larger notes.
- **Ticket Types:**
  - **Single Journey Ticket:** This is the most common and cheapest option, valid for a one-way trip.
  - **Day Passes:** Available for travelers who plan to use the bus frequently in a single day, offering unlimited travel within a 24-hour period. These passes are available for purchase at larger stations.
  - **Monthly or Weekly Passes:** If you're staying in Tunis for an extended period, monthly or weekly passes may be a convenient and cost-effective option. These can be purchased from specific locations or online, and they provide unlimited travel within a given period.

Bus Stops and Terminals

- **Main Bus Terminals:**
  - **Bab el Bhar (Porte de France):** Located in the heart of the city, this is one of the busiest and most important bus hubs. It's a central point for many routes connecting various parts of Tunis.

- ○ **Tunis Marine:** This terminal serves as a major transit point, especially for travelers heading toward the northern parts of the city and suburban areas.
  - ○ **Ariana Bus Station:** A key stop for those traveling to the nearby Ariana district, offering good connectivity to central Tunis.

- **Bus Stops:**
  - ○ Bus stops are usually marked with clear signage, featuring the route numbers and a list of destinations. These can be found at most major intersections, as well as in residential areas.
  - ○ At smaller stops, schedules may not be as easily available, so it's best to rely on local knowledge or ask passersby for information.

Travel Tips for Using Buses in Tunis

- **Avoiding Peak Hours:**
  - ○ As with most major cities, Tunis buses can get crowded during peak hours (7:00 AM – 9:00 AM and 5:00 PM – 7:00 PM). Try to plan your travel during off-peak hours to avoid the rush.
- **Be Prepared for Delays:**
  - ○ While buses in Tunis are generally reliable, delays can occasionally occur, especially during heavy traffic or bad weather. Allow extra time for your journey if you have a time-sensitive appointment.
- **Safety and Security:**
  - ○ Keep an eye on your belongings while traveling, as buses can sometimes attract pickpockets, especially during crowded trips.

- o When traveling at night, consider using a taxi or ridesharing app for added security.
- **Language Tips:**
  - o While Arabic is the official language, many bus drivers and passengers also speak French. If you're not fluent in either language, it can be helpful to learn a few key phrases such as "Où est la station de bus?" (Where is the bus station?) or "Combien ça coûte?" (How much does it cost?).

Metro Light Rail (Métro Léger)

Tunis is home to an efficient and modern metro light rail network known as the **Métro Léger**, which serves as one of the most convenient and affordable ways to get around the city. This public transit option is particularly useful for travelers who wish to avoid traffic or need to cover longer distances within the urban area. The **Métro Léger** connects central Tunis to various suburban neighborhoods, making it an essential part of daily life for locals and an invaluable tool for visitors.

Overview of the Metro Light Rail (Métro Léger)

The Métro Léger network consists of six main lines that cover a large portion of the Greater Tunis area, offering fast, reliable, and eco-friendly travel. The metro system is operated by the Société des Transports de Tunis (TRANSTU), the same organization that oversees the city's bus network.

- **Lines and Coverage:**

- **Line 1**: Running from the Tunis Marine station in the city center to El Mourouj, this line connects key areas such as Place Mongi Slim and Bab El Khadra.
- **Line 2**: Connecting Tunis Marine to Ariana, Line 2 passes through popular districts like Bab Saadoun and Place de la République.
- **Line 3**: The shortest metro line, linking Cité El Khadra to La Goulette, a coastal town near Tunis.
- **Line 4**: Running from Tunis Marine to Ben Arous, this line connects several busy commercial and residential areas.
- **Line 5**: Connecting the central Tunis Marine area to Sidi Hsan, an important route for daily commuters.
- **Line 6**: Serving the eastern parts of the city, including districts like Cité Ennasr, and extending toward La Marsa.

These metro lines connect with several other transportation networks in Tunis, such as buses, taxis, and the train service, providing easy and efficient transit options for visitors and residents alike.

Key Features of the Metro Light Rail System

- **Frequency and Operating Hours:**
  - **Métro Léger** trains operate from 5:30 AM to 10:00 PM, making them a convenient choice for early morning or late-evening travel.
  - During peak hours (7:00–9:00 AM and 5:00–7:00 PM), the metro runs at frequent intervals, typically every 7 to 10 minutes. During off-peak times, trains may arrive every 15–20 minutes.

- **Speed and Efficiency:**
    - The Métro Léger is designed for speed and efficiency. It bypasses the traffic congestion that often affects buses and taxis, allowing travelers to reach their destinations quickly and reliably.
    - The metro is particularly useful for commuters heading to business districts, the central business hub, or tourist attractions like Carthage and Sidi Bou Said.
- **Stations and Accessibility:**
    - Stations are well-maintained and typically located near major transit points, shopping areas, residential neighborhoods, and important landmarks.
    - **Tunis Marine** is the central hub, and other major stations include Bab El Khadra, Cité El Khadra, and La Marsa.
    - **Metro stations** are generally accessible for people with disabilities, with low-floor trains and ramps at platforms to facilitate easy boarding.

Ticketing and Fares

The Métro Léger offers a simple and affordable ticketing system, with fares based on the distance traveled. Tickets can be purchased at stations via automated machines, ticket booths, or kiosks. Passengers should purchase their tickets before boarding the train.

- **Ticket Prices:**
    - A standard one-way ticket typically costs around 0.5 to 1 Tunisian dinar (TND) for a short journey.
    - Longer distances or routes extending to suburban areas may cost slightly more, but the fares remain

reasonably low compared to other modes of transportation.
- **Day passes** and **monthly passes** are available for travelers who plan to use the metro frequently. These passes offer unlimited travel on the metro, making them a great choice for tourists staying in the city for a few days or longer.
- **Ticket Types:**
  - **Single Journey Ticket:** A one-way ticket for short trips within the city.
  - **Return Ticket:** A ticket for round-trip journeys within the same day.
  - **Day Pass:** Provides unlimited travel on the metro for one day.
  - **Monthly Pass:** Ideal for longer stays or those traveling frequently on the metro.
- **Payment Methods:**
  - Tickets can be purchased with cash or credit/debit cards at the stations. Many machines are equipped with both Arabic and French instructions, making it easier for tourists to navigate the ticketing process.

Safety and Security

The Métro Léger is considered to be a safe and secure mode of transport in Tunis. However, as with any busy urban transit system, passengers should remain aware of their surroundings.

- **Safety Measures:**
  - **CCTV cameras** are installed in stations and on trains, and security personnel are present at key points to ensure safety.

- o **Police patrols** are common, especially during peak travel times.
- **Travel Tips:**
  - o **Keep an eye on your belongings**: While the metro is generally safe, like any other public transport, pickpockets can be active, especially during crowded periods.
  - o If you are traveling during peak hours, be prepared for **crowded trains**, particularly in the central parts of the city.

How to Use the Metro Light Rail

1. **Buying a Ticket:** Once you arrive at a metro station, head to one of the ticket machines or kiosks to purchase your ticket. Select your destination on the map if using a machine or ask the staff if you're unsure of your fare.
2. **Boarding the Train:** At the platform, check the train's route number and ensure it's heading in the right direction. Each station has clear signage in both Arabic and French, indicating train routes and destinations.
3. **Onboard Etiquette:**
   - o **Seats are available** for those who need them, but during rush hours, standing may be necessary.
   - o **Priority seating** is given to elderly passengers and those with disabilities.
4. **Exiting the Train:** At your destination, exit through the doors marked with green signs. Be prepared to present your ticket to station staff if asked.

Travel Tips for Using the Metro Light Rail in Tunis

- **Avoid Peak Hours:** Trains are most crowded during morning and evening rush hours (7:00–9:00 AM and 5:00–7:00 PM). If possible, plan your travel outside of these busy times for a more comfortable experience.
- **Stay Hydrated:** Tunis can get quite hot, especially in summer. If you're traveling during the warmer months, carry a bottle of water with you. Many stations have vending machines where you can purchase refreshments.
- **Keep a Metro Map Handy:** Maps of the metro system are available at stations and on the official TRANSTU website. Familiarizing yourself with the route map can make navigating the system easier.

Taxis in Tunis

Taxis are widely available in Tunis, and they provide a convenient and often preferred means of transportation for both locals and tourists. There are two main types of taxis in the city: **regular taxis** and **grand taxis**.

Types of Taxis

- **Regular Taxis (Petite Taxis):**
    - **Description:** The most common type of taxi in Tunis, these are yellow and black cars with a "TAXI" sign on the roof. They are small, typically seating up to four passengers, and are perfect for short trips around the city.
    - **Fare System:** The fare for regular taxis is based on a metered system, which means the price starts at a base rate and increases based on the distance traveled. The meter is required to be on, and the

starting fare is typically around 1.3 TND, with an additional 0.6 TND per kilometer.
- **Availability:** Regular taxis can be hailed on the street, found at designated taxi ranks, or booked by phone. They are generally available at major tourist spots, hotels, and transport hubs such as the Tunis-Carthage Airport and Tunis Marine station.
- **Payment:** Cash is the most common payment method, although some taxis may accept credit or debit cards, particularly those that cater to tourists. It is advisable to ask the driver beforehand if they accept card payments.

- **Grand Taxis (Taxis Collectifs):**
  - **Description:** Larger than regular taxis, grand taxis are typically white vehicles and can carry up to six passengers. They are used for longer journeys, especially to suburban areas or neighboring cities like La Marsa or Carthage.
  - **Fare System:** Grand taxis operate on a fixed fare basis for longer distances, and prices are often negotiated before departure. Fares to neighboring towns or suburbs generally range from 10 to 25 TND depending on the distance.
  - **Availability:** Grand taxis are typically available at major bus stations or transport terminals and are especially useful for travelers heading out of the city center or to more distant parts of the greater Tunis area.
  - **Payment:** Similar to regular taxis, payments are made in cash, and prices should be agreed upon before departure.

Taxi Travel Tips

- **Always Use the Meter:** For regular taxis, insist that the driver turns on the meter at the start of your ride. If the driver refuses or claims the meter is broken, it's best to walk away and look for another taxi.
- **Confirm the Fare for Longer Rides:** If you're taking a **grand taxi** or a taxi for a longer journey outside of the city center, it's a good idea to agree on a fare before you begin the ride. This avoids misunderstandings when you reach your destination.
- **Check the Taxi's Identification:** Ensure the taxi has a visible taxi registration number and the driver's identification before getting into the vehicle. This can be helpful if any issues arise.
- **Language:** Most taxi drivers speak Arabic and French. However, basic English phrases are often understood in tourist-heavy areas. It's helpful to learn a few key phrases.

Ride-Sharing Services in Tunis

In addition to traditional taxis, ride-sharing services have become increasingly popular in Tunis, offering a more modern, user-friendly alternative for getting around the city. Services such as Uber, Bolt, and Yassir have expanded in Tunis, providing tourists with an easy way to book rides via smartphone apps.

Uber in Tunis

- **Overview:** Uber is available in Tunis and operates similarly to other cities around the world. The service is

widely used by tourists and locals alike for its ease of use and transparency in pricing.
- **Booking:** To use Uber, you'll need to download the **Uber app** on your smartphone and set up an account. Once you've entered your destination, the app will show you a fare estimate, and you can choose your preferred vehicle type (UberX, UberXL, etc.).
- **Fare System:** Unlike traditional taxis, Uber fares are calculated based on the distance and time, and the price is displayed before you confirm the ride. This system removes any confusion about pricing and ensures that you're not overcharged.
- **Payment:** Payment for Uber rides is made cashlessly through the app, either via credit/debit card or PayPal, which makes it convenient for travelers who don't want to carry cash.
- **Availability:** Uber operates throughout the city of Tunis, including major tourist areas, hotels, and the airport. However, availability may vary during peak times or in more remote locations.

Bolt in Tunis

- **Overview:** Bolt, a ride-sharing app that operates in various countries, is also present in Tunis. It is often favored for its competitive pricing and ease of use, providing another option for tourists who are familiar with the app.
- **Booking:** Like Uber, you can use the Bolt app to book a ride to your destination. Once the ride is booked, you'll be able to track your driver's arrival in real time.

- **Fare System:** Bolt's pricing is based on distance and time, and you'll receive an upfront fare estimate when you book your ride.
- **Payment:** Payment is handled through the app, using credit/debit cards or mobile payment systems like Apple Pay. Cash payment is not typically available.
- **Availability:** Bolt operates across **Tunis**, including major routes to and from the airport and tourist sites. Similar to Uber, the availability of rides may vary depending on the time of day.

Yassir in Tunis

- **Overview:** Yassir is a popular local ride-sharing service that has gained traction in Tunis. It offers an alternative to the global services like Uber and Bolt, and many local residents use it for everyday commuting.
- **Booking:** Yassir is accessed through the **Yassir app**, where you can enter your pickup and drop-off locations. The app will provide you with an estimated fare before you confirm the ride.
- **Fare System:** Yassir uses the distance and time system, with transparent pricing provided upfront.
- **Payment:** Similar to Uber and Bolt, Yassir allows cashless payments via the app using credit/debit cards or mobile wallets. Cash payments are also accepted in some cases.
- **Availability:** Yassir is available across Tunis and serves both residential areas and tourist spots. As it is a local service, it may be more widely used by Tunis residents than tourists, but it remains a reliable option for travel.

Benefits of Ride-Sharing Services

- **Convenience:** Ride-sharing services like Uber, Bolt, and Yassir are incredibly convenient, allowing you to book rides directly from your smartphone without needing to hail a taxi or navigate a foreign city's public transportation system.
- **Pricing Transparency:** One of the biggest advantages of using ride-sharing services is price transparency. You'll know the fare upfront, so you don't have to worry about being overcharged, especially for longer rides.
- **Cashless Transactions:** Payments are handled directly through the app, which means you don't have to worry about carrying cash or fumbling for change during your ride.
- **Language Barrier:** Many ride-sharing drivers are familiar with English, which can be helpful for non-Arabic-speaking tourists. If you have trouble explaining your destination, the app allows you to type in the address, which makes communication easier.

Car Rentals in Tunis

Several international and local car rental agencies operate in Tunis, providing a range of vehicles to suit various needs and budgets. Renting a car can be a convenient option for travelers looking to move independently and explore the area without relying on taxis or public transportation.

Car Rental Agencies in Tunis

- **International Car Rental Companies:**
    - **Hertz**, **Europcar**, **Avis**, and **Budget** are some of the international car rental companies with offices

in Tunis. These companies often have locations at the **Tunis-Carthage International Airport** and within the city center, making it easy to pick up and drop off your rental car.
    - **Benefits**: International companies typically offer higher levels of customer service, a broad selection of vehicles, and guaranteed quality standards. They often have a strong online presence, which can be helpful for booking in advance.
- **Local Car Rental Companies:**
    - In addition to international chains, there are numerous local rental agencies in Tunis, such as Sixt Tunisia, Tunisia Rent Car, and Inter Rent Tunisia. Local agencies often offer more competitive rates and may provide a more personalized experience, but they may not have the same level of consistency in service.
    - **Benefits**: Local agencies often have a variety of smaller, more affordable cars that may be more suited to tourists on a budget.

Types of Vehicles Available for Rent

- **Economy Cars**: These are ideal for solo travelers or couples. They are affordable and fuel-efficient, making them a popular choice for tourists who plan to stay within the city or make short trips.
- **Compact Cars**: Perfect for small families or groups of friends, these vehicles offer more space than economy cars while still being easy to maneuver through Tunisian streets.
- **SUVs and 4x4s**: These are the best option for those looking to explore the countryside or visit areas with rougher roads.

They are also a good choice for families or groups who require more luggage space.
- **Luxury Cars**: Some rental agencies in Tunis also offer luxury vehicles for those wanting a more comfortable and stylish travel experience.
- **Minivans**: Suitable for larger groups or families, minivans provide plenty of space for passengers and luggage.

Booking a Car in Tunis

Car rentals in Tunis can be arranged in advance via the company's website, or you can book directly at the rental agency's office upon arrival. Booking in advance is recommended, especially during the high tourist season (April to October), as it ensures better availability and often allows you to secure a better price.

- **Required Documents for Rental:**
    - **Passport**: International tourists will need to show their passport.
    - **Driver's License**: You'll need a valid driver's license from your home country. If your license is not in French or Arabic, an International Driver's Permit (IDP) may be required.
    - **Credit Card**: A credit card in the driver's name is generally required for security and payment purposes. Most rental agencies will place a hold on your card as a deposit.
    - **Age Requirements**: Renters must generally be at least 21 years old (with some agencies requiring a minimum age of 25), and those under 25 may incur an additional young driver fee. Additionally, most

agencies require a minimum of 1–2 years of driving experience.
- **Booking Tips**:
  - **Compare Prices**: Different agencies may offer different rates, so it's worthwhile to compare prices on websites like Kayak, Rentalcars, or Expedia.
  - **Look for Deals**: Many rental companies offer promotions for longer rentals, early bookings, or discounted weekend rates.
  - **Check for Additional Fees**: Always clarify the total cost, including any potential insurance charges, fuel policies, or drop-off fees. Some rental agencies charge extra if you return the car with an empty fuel tank.

Driving in Tunis

Driving in Tunis and Tunisia at large can be a rewarding experience, but it comes with a unique set of challenges. To ensure your trip is smooth and enjoyable, it's important to familiarize yourself with local driving customs, road conditions, and traffic rules.

Road Conditions

- **City Roads**: In central Tunis, major roads are generally in good condition, and you'll find paved streets in most urban areas. However, some side streets may be narrow and poorly lit, especially in older parts of the city. Driving within the Medina (Old Town) can be particularly tricky due to narrow, winding streets, so be prepared for more careful maneuvering if you're headed in that direction.

- **Highways**: Major highways, such as those leading from Tunis to the coastal towns or inland areas, are generally in good condition and well-maintained. Some roads leading to more remote areas might be less well-kept, especially in rural or mountainous regions.
- **Parking**: Parking in downtown Tunis can be challenging, especially during peak hours. It is advisable to use designated parking areas or hotel parking. If you're planning to park on the street, be aware of local parking rules to avoid fines or towing.

Traffic and Driving Culture

- **Traffic Flow**: Traffic in Tunis can be quite busy, particularly during rush hours (7:30 AM–9:00 AM and 5:00 PM–7:00 PM). Expect heavy congestion on major routes, and be aware that traffic laws may not always be strictly followed, especially by local drivers.
- **Driving Style**: Tunisian drivers tend to be aggressive and fast-paced, with frequent lane changes and limited respect for traffic signals. It's important to drive defensively, anticipate the actions of other drivers, and be prepared for sudden stops.
- **Pedestrian Crossings**: Pedestrian crossings are often ignored by vehicles, so always be cautious when walking across the road.
- **Roundabouts**: Roundabouts are common in Tunis, and the general rule is that vehicles inside the roundabout have the right of way. However, this may not always be observed, so exercise caution when approaching or entering roundabouts.

Traffic Rules and Regulations

- **Speed Limits**:
    - In **urban areas**, the speed limit is generally **50 km/h**.
    - On **highways**, the limit is typically **90 km/h** to **110 km/h**, depending on the road.
    - Always check for posted speed limit signs, as these can vary.
- **Seat Belts**: The use of **seat belts** is mandatory for all passengers. Fines can be imposed for non-compliance.
- **Mobile Phones**: Using a **mobile phone** while driving without a hands-free device is prohibited. Avoid distractions and focus on the road.
- **Alcohol Limits**: The legal **blood alcohol limit** is 0.02%. While this is quite low, it's advisable to avoid alcohol altogether when driving.

Navigation and Local Road Signs

- **Road Signs**: Road signs in Tunisia are generally in Arabic and French, and in larger cities, you'll also find some signs in English. Familiarizing yourself with common road signs can be helpful.
- **GPS and Maps**: Using a **GPS device** or navigation apps like **Google Maps** or **Waze** is highly recommended to avoid getting lost, especially in unfamiliar neighborhoods.

Fuel and Refueling

- **Fuel Stations**: Fuel is widely available throughout Tunis, and you can find **petrol stations** in the city as well as along major highways. Gasoline (super) and diesel are both

commonly used. Credit cards are accepted at most stations, although it's always good to carry **cash** in case you encounter a station that doesn't accept cards.
- **Fuel Prices**: Gasoline prices in Tunisia are relatively affordable compared to many Western countries. However, they can fluctuate based on global market prices, so it's a good idea to check the current rates before filling up.

Driving Tips for Tourists

- **Driving Hours**: Stick to driving during daylight hours for better visibility. Roads can be poorly lit in some areas, and driving at night can be more challenging.
- **Avoid Rush Hour**: If possible, avoid traveling during **rush hour** to minimize your time spent in traffic.
- **Local Drivers**: Be prepared for local drivers who may not always obey traffic laws. Stay alert and maintain a safe distance from other vehicles.

Walking Around Tunis

Tunis, the bustling capital of Tunisia, offers a rich blend of history, culture, and modern life, making it a fascinating destination for those who enjoy walking tours. Exploring the city on foot allows you to immerse yourself in the atmosphere of its narrow streets, markets, and vibrant neighborhoods. Whether you're wandering through the ancient Medina, strolling along the Avenue Habib Bourguiba, or discovering the city's hidden gems, walking is one of the best ways to experience the local culture and interact with residents.

Essential Tips for Walking Around Tunis

- **Wear Comfortable Shoes**: The streets of Tunis can be uneven, especially in the older areas like the **Medina**. Comfortable, sturdy shoes are essential for a day of walking. Sandals with straps or sneakers are ideal for navigating both cobblestones and paved roads.
- **Stay Hydrated**: Tunis can get hot, particularly in the summer months. Carry a bottle of water with you, especially if you plan on walking for an extended period. Many cafes and small shops sell bottled water if you need to top up.
- **Sun Protection**: The sun in Tunis can be intense, especially from April to October. Wear **sunscreen**, a **hat**, and **sunglasses** to protect yourself from sunburn.
- **Be Mindful of Traffic**: Although Tunis has a relatively good pedestrian infrastructure, traffic can be unpredictable, particularly in busy areas. Always cross streets at marked pedestrian crossings, but remain cautious of vehicles, as not all drivers will yield to pedestrians.
- **Plan Your Route**: Tunis has several districts, each offering a unique experience. Make sure to plan your walking route according to what you want to see and where you're going. Some areas, such as the **Medina**, are best explored on foot, while others, like **La Marsa** or **Sidi Bou Said**, are further out and may require other forms of transport for convenience.

Walking Safety and Etiquette in Tunis

- **Street Vendors and Beggars**: Be prepared for interactions with street vendors who will try to sell you goods. It's

advisable to politely refuse if you're not interested. Similarly, you may encounter beggars, especially near busy areas like the Medina.
- **Local Etiquette**: Tunisians are generally friendly and welcoming. When greeting someone on the street, a simple "Salam Alaikum" (peace be upon you) or "Bonjour" (hello) in French is appreciated.
- **Pickpocketing**: While Tunis is relatively safe, pickpocketing can occur, particularly in crowded areas like the Medina or markets. Keep your valuables secure, avoid displaying large amounts of cash, and be cautious with your belongings.

In conclusion, getting around Tunis is convenient and diverse, offering a range of transportation options to suit every traveler's needs. From the efficient Metro Light Rail and extensive bus network to taxis, ride-sharing services, and car rentals, there are plenty of ways to navigate the city comfortably. Walking through its vibrant neighborhoods, such as the Medina or Avenue Habib Bourguiba, allows visitors to soak in the local culture at a slower pace. Whether you prefer the hustle of public transport or the flexibility of a rental car, Tunis provides an accessible and engaging travel experience.

ACCOMMODATION OPTIONS IN TUNIS

Tunis offers a diverse range of accommodation options that cater to various budgets and preferences, from opulent hotels to charming boutique stays and budget-friendly hostels. Here's a comprehensive guide to help you choose the perfect place to stay while visiting the Tunisian capital.

Luxury Hotels in Tunis

For travelers who wish to indulge in the finest comforts during their stay in Tunis, the city offers a selection of luxurious hotels that combine sophisticated style, impeccable service, and world-class amenities. Whether you are looking for a beachfront resort, a stylish city retreat, or a historic hotel with modern upgrades, Tunis has a luxury option to suit your needs.

The Residence Tunis

A serene oasis located on the beach, The Residence Tunis is one of the top luxury hotels in Tunis. This five-star property blends traditional Tunisian architecture with modern comforts. The hotel offers an exclusive atmosphere with expansive gardens, a private beach, and state-of-the-art facilities.

Key Features:

- **Beachfront Location**: The hotel boasts direct access to a private sandy beach, perfect for sunbathing or enjoying water activities.

- **Wellness and Spa**: The Six Senses Spa offers a wide range of treatments including massages, body wraps, and facials, set within a peaceful environment.
- **Golf Course**: Guests can enjoy the 18-hole golf course designed by renowned architect Robert Trent Jones.
- **Dining**: The hotel features several dining options, including a fine-dining restaurant with views of the Mediterranean Sea, offering Tunisian and international cuisine.

Why Choose It: The Residence Tunis is ideal for those who want a luxurious, relaxing retreat with world-class amenities and a beachfront location. The serene atmosphere makes it perfect for families, couples, and anyone looking for a tranquil escape.

Laico Tunis

Situated in the heart of Tunis, Laico Tunis is a prestigious luxury hotel that combines modern amenities with traditional Tunisian hospitality. Located close to business districts, shopping centers, and cultural attractions, this hotel is a popular choice for both business and leisure travelers.

Key Features:

- **Central Location**: Just a short drive from the city center and the Medina, Laico Tunis offers convenient access to major landmarks.
- **Rooms and Suites**: Spacious rooms decorated with plush furniture and luxurious fabrics. The suites include large living spaces, private balconies, and stunning views of the city.

- **Spa and Wellness**: The hotel offers a full-service spa with a variety of treatments, an indoor swimming pool, a sauna, and a fitness center.
- **Gastronomy**: Guests can enjoy fine dining at the hotel's restaurant, which serves a blend of Tunisian and Mediterranean cuisine. The hotel also offers an elegant bar and café for casual dining.

Why Choose It: Laico Tunis is perfect for travelers who want a luxurious experience with a central location. Its proximity to both business and tourist hubs makes it an excellent option for those visiting Tunis for work or pleasure.

Sheraton Tunis Hotel & Towers

A symbol of luxury and sophistication in the Tunisian capital, the Sheraton Tunis Hotel & Towers is renowned for its exceptional service and facilities. Set on the hills overlooking the city, it offers sweeping views of Tunis, with easy access to the city's attractions.

Key Features:

- **Panoramic Views**: The hotel's elevated location provides breathtaking views of the Tunisian landscape, including the Mediterranean Sea and the city.
- **Rooms and Suites**: The rooms and suites are tastefully designed with luxurious touches and modern conveniences. The Tower Suites offer added exclusivity and premium services for elite travelers.
- **Outdoor Pool**: The hotel features a large outdoor pool with a deck for lounging and sunbathing.
- **Dining and Bars**: The hotel offers a selection of dining venues, including an international buffet restaurant, a

Moroccan-style eatery, and a chic bar with a stunning view of the city.

Why Choose It: Ideal for business travelers, couples, and those looking to enjoy Tunis from an elevated perspective, the Sheraton Tunis Hotel & Towers delivers luxurious accommodations, excellent service, and stunning views of the capital.

Four Seasons Hotel Tunis

The Four Seasons Hotel Tunis is the epitome of luxury and modern design. With a location that blends city convenience and seaside tranquility, it is perfect for those who want to combine cultural exploration with a luxurious resort experience.

Key Features:

- **Seaside Resort**: Located on the beach, the Four Seasons offers a beautiful private shoreline with water sports, poolside lounging, and stunning sunsets.
- **Exclusive Spa**: The hotel's spa offers traditional Tunisian treatments combined with modern wellness therapies. Guests can enjoy hammams, facials, massages, and more in a serene environment.
- **Culinary Excellence**: The hotel features high-end dining with Mediterranean and Tunisian-inspired dishes, served in an elegant atmosphere.
- **Family-Friendly Services**: The Four Seasons offers dedicated family services, including kids' clubs, family suites, and babysitting services, making it an ideal choice for families.

Why Choose It: Perfect for those who want a beachside luxury experience with access to the best amenities, the Four Seasons Hotel Tunis provides a luxurious escape with a mix of cultural exploration and resort relaxation.

Mövenpick Hotel du Lac Tunis

Located by Lake Tunis, the Mövenpick Hotel du Lac combines modern luxury with refined elegance. Known for its superb service and prime location, this hotel caters to both business and leisure travelers seeking a peaceful retreat in a luxurious setting.

Key Features:

- **Lakeside Views**: The hotel offers scenic views of Lake Tunis, providing a tranquil atmosphere away from the hustle and bustle of the city.
- **Modern Design**: The Mövenpick Hotel is designed with sleek, contemporary furnishings and offers spacious, well-equipped rooms and suites.
- **Wellness Facilities**: The hotel has a modern fitness center, a spa, and an outdoor swimming pool, making it ideal for relaxation and rejuvenation.
- **Dining Options**: Mövenpick offers a range of dining experiences, including international cuisine, Mediterranean fare, and local Tunisian dishes, with a focus on fresh ingredients and quality.

Why Choose It: This hotel is perfect for those looking for a luxurious stay with lakeside tranquility, modern amenities, and proximity to Tunis' business districts. It is ideal for guests seeking peace and comfort with easy access to city attractions.

Boutique Hotels in Tunis

Boutique hotels in Tunis offer travelers a more personalized, intimate experience compared to larger chain hotels. These smaller, independent accommodations are known for their unique character, attention to detail, and exceptional service. Often situated in historical buildings or residential neighborhoods, boutique hotels in Tunis allow guests to experience the local culture while enjoying modern comforts. Here are some of the top boutique hotel options in Tunis that stand out for their charm, atmosphere, and individuality.

Dar Ben Gacem

Situated in the heart of the Medina, Dar Ben Gacem offers an authentic Tunisian experience in a beautifully restored traditional house. The architecture reflects the old-world charm of Tunis, with intricate mosaics, hand-carved woodwork, and original features that create a warm, welcoming atmosphere.

Key Features:

- **Authentic Traditional Style**: The hotel's decor is a perfect blend of Tunisian heritage, showcasing intricate designs and traditional furnishings. Each room is uniquely styled, offering a blend of old-world charm with modern amenities.
- **Intimate and Personalized Experience**: With only a few rooms, Dar Ben Gacem offers a quiet, intimate stay with highly personalized service. Guests are treated like family and can expect genuine hospitality.

- **Location**: Situated just steps away from the bustling souks of the Medina, Dar Ben Gacem offers easy access to key attractions such as the Zitouna Mosque, the Bardo Museum, and local artisan shops.
- **Private Courtyard**: The hotel features a beautiful internal courtyard, ideal for enjoying a peaceful moment with a cup of mint tea or a traditional Tunisian breakfast.

Why Choose It: Perfect for travelers looking for an authentic, immersive stay in the heart of Tunis' historic Medina. The traditional atmosphere combined with a small, personal service makes it ideal for those wanting to experience Tunisian culture up close.

Dar El Medina

This family-run boutique hotel offers a blend of traditional Tunisian hospitality and modern design. Set in a beautifully renovated 18th-century house, Dar El Medina provides a unique opportunity to stay in the heart of the old city while enjoying contemporary comforts.

Key Features:

- **Traditional Elegance**: The hotel is a blend of contemporary and traditional Tunisian styles, with tiled floors, carved wooden details, and luxurious fabrics. Each room is designed with unique touches, creating a sense of elegance and comfort.
- **Private and Peaceful Atmosphere**: With only a handful of rooms, the hotel ensures a serene atmosphere, allowing guests to unwind and relax in an intimate setting.

- **Proximity to Key Sites**: Located within the Medina, it offers easy access to landmarks such as the Medina's souks, the Zitouna Mosque, and the Carthage Museum.
- **Roof Terrace**: Guests can enjoy breathtaking views of the Medina and beyond from the hotel's rooftop terrace. The perfect place to enjoy the sunset or relax in the evenings with a drink.

Why Choose It: For those who want to experience Tunisian life in a traditional yet modern setting, Dar El Medina offers an ideal location and ambiance. The blend of comfort, style, and historical charm makes it an excellent choice for travelers seeking a unique, intimate stay.

Maison d'hôtes Dar Ennassim

A peaceful and elegant Riad located in the heart of the Medina, Dar Ennassim is a charming guesthouse offering guests a quiet retreat within the vibrant historical center of Tunis. This boutique hotel is perfect for those who want to escape the hustle and bustle of the city while being close to key attractions.

Key Features:

- **Traditional Tunisian Architecture**: The interior of Dar Ennassim is designed in the traditional Tunisian style, with ornate arches, intricate tilework, and wooden furnishings that evoke the city's rich history.
- **Personalized Service**: The staff at Dar Ennassim offers warm, attentive service, with a focus on creating a personalized experience for each guest.

- **Central Location**: Nestled within the Medina, it is a short walk from major attractions like the Zitouna Mosque, souks, and the Bardo Museum.
- **Tranquil Courtyard**: Guests can relax in the peaceful inner courtyard, which offers a calming atmosphere to enjoy meals, tea, or simply unwind.

Why Choose It: Dar Ennassim is perfect for those seeking a more peaceful and personalized experience in the Medina. Its quiet, elegant setting and attentive service make it a great choice for couples or solo travelers looking for an intimate and relaxing stay.

Villa Didon

For travelers seeking something a bit more modern while still maintaining a sense of intimacy, Villa Didon offers luxury and comfort in a boutique setting. Overlooking the Mediterranean Sea, this boutique hotel combines sleek design with a cozy, homely feel.

Key Features:

- **Modern Design with Views**: Villa Didon's chic, minimalist design is complemented by panoramic views of the Mediterranean. The hotel's modern architecture includes large windows and open spaces, providing guests with a bright, airy atmosphere.
- **Exclusive Atmosphere**: With only a limited number of rooms, Villa Didon offers an exclusive experience where every guest receives exceptional attention.
- **Private Pool and Spa**: The hotel features a beautiful outdoor pool and a small but well-equipped spa where guests can enjoy treatments and massages.

- **Fine Dining**: The hotel's restaurant offers Mediterranean-inspired dishes, made with fresh, local ingredients, and served with an emphasis on quality and flavor.

Why Choose It: Villa Didon is perfect for travelers who prefer modern comfort and exclusivity. Its coastal views and stylish atmosphere make it ideal for those seeking a luxurious, yet intimate experience.

The Medina Hostel and Boutique

For travelers on a more modest budget but still looking for a boutique-style stay, The Medina Hostel and Boutique offers a unique experience with its combination of stylish interiors and affordable pricing.

Key Features:

- **Modern Boutique Design**: The Medina Hostel offers a blend of chic, contemporary design with traditional Tunisian elements. Its minimalist decor combined with traditional touches creates a modern yet cozy environment.
- **Social Atmosphere**: Despite being a hostel, The Medina offers a boutique vibe with a communal lounge, perfect for meeting other travelers.
- **Location**: Set just outside the Medina, the hostel is close enough to walk to the souks, museums, and restaurants, making it an ideal base for exploring Tunis.
- **Affordable and Comfortable**: With both dormitory and private rooms, The Medina offers budget-friendly accommodation without sacrificing style or comfort.

Why Choose It: The Medina Hostel and Boutique is a great option for travelers looking for budget-friendly accommodation with a touch of style. It's a great option for young travelers, backpackers, or those seeking a social, intimate environment on a smaller budget.

Mid-Range and Budget Hotels in Tunis

Tunis offers a range of mid-range and budget hotel options that combine great value with essential comforts, making them an excellent choice for travelers who want a quality experience without overspending. These hotels offer clean, comfortable rooms, central locations, and affordable prices, perfect for tourists who prioritize comfort, convenience, and cost-effectiveness. Here are some of the top picks for mid-range and budget hotels in Tunis that promise a memorable stay without breaking the bank.

Ibis Tunis

As part of the internationally recognized Ibis chain, Ibis Tunis offers a modern, no-frills experience for travelers looking for affordable comfort. Located in a convenient area near Tunis' business districts and tourist attractions, it is perfect for both business and leisure travelers.

Key Features:

- **Convenient Location**: Situated near the Belvedere Park and within easy reach of the city center, the hotel offers quick access to Tunis' main sights, including the Medina and the Bardo Museum.
- **Modern Rooms**: Rooms are simple, clean, and modern, equipped with comfortable bedding, air conditioning, free Wi-Fi, and flat-screen TVs.

- **Restaurant and Bar**: The hotel's on-site restaurant serves international dishes, and guests can unwind at the cozy bar after a busy day of sightseeing or meetings.
- **Affordable Pricing**: Offering competitive rates, Ibis Tunis is one of the most budget-friendly options in its category, without sacrificing comfort and quality.

Why Choose It: Ideal for travelers who are looking for a straightforward, reliable, and budget-friendly stay with easy access to the city's attractions and business centers. The combination of value and convenience makes Ibis Tunis a top choice.

Hotel Africa

Hotel Africa is a mid-range hotel that offers excellent value for money, located in the heart of Tunis. Its prime location near the city center makes it a popular choice for travelers who want easy access to both business areas and cultural attractions.

Key Features:

- **Great Location**: Hotel Africa is located just minutes away from the central business district and the Medina, making it perfect for those who want to explore the city's rich culture and history.
- **Comfortable Rooms**: The hotel offers comfortable rooms with modern amenities, such as air conditioning, cable TV, and free Wi-Fi. Rooms come in various sizes, including family-friendly options.
- **On-Site Dining**: The hotel features an on-site restaurant offering Tunisian and Mediterranean cuisine, allowing guests to enjoy local flavors without leaving the property.

- **Friendly Service**: The hotel's staff is known for their attentive service, offering recommendations for nearby attractions and activities.

Why Choose It: With its central location, excellent value for money, and comfortable amenities, Hotel Africa is ideal for travelers looking for a well-rounded mid-range option in the heart of Tunis.

El Mouradi Hotel

El Mouradi Hotel offers a fantastic mid-range option for those seeking both comfort and affordability. Located near the city's business districts and the Mediterranean coast, it provides a convenient location for business travelers and tourists alike.

Key Features:

- **Affordable Comfort**: The hotel offers a variety of rooms, ranging from standard rooms to more spacious suites, all equipped with air conditioning, satellite TV, and free Wi-Fi.
- **Facilities**: El Mouradi Hotel has a large outdoor pool, fitness center, and spa services, offering guests plenty of options for relaxation and recreation.
- **Restaurant and Cafés**: Guests can enjoy Tunisian and international dishes at the hotel's restaurant, with several cafés and bars available for snacks or drinks throughout the day.

- **Proximity to Attractions**: The hotel is close to cultural landmarks like the Medina and Bardo Museum, as well as the beautiful beaches of La Marsa.

Why Choose It: El Mouradi Hotel is a great choice for those looking for a mid-range hotel with a full range of amenities, including leisure facilities, while maintaining an affordable price point.

Hotel Carlton

Hotel Carlton is a budget-friendly, centrally located option in Tunis that offers a welcoming atmosphere, ideal for tourists on a budget. Set in a historic building, it provides easy access to key attractions such as the Medina, Avenue Habib Bourguiba, and the historic old town.

Key Features:

- **Central Location**: Located on Avenue Habib Bourguiba, one of Tunis' main streets, Hotel Carlton is close to the city's shops, restaurants, and major attractions.
- **Charming Rooms**: The hotel's rooms are simple but comfortable, with traditional décor, air conditioning, free Wi-Fi, and TV. Many rooms also offer views of the bustling avenue or the nearby Old City.
- **Affordable Rates**: Offering competitive rates, Hotel Carlton is a great budget option for travelers who need a basic place to stay without compromising on location.
- **Breakfast Buffet**: The hotel offers a continental breakfast buffet to start your day with a selection of fresh pastries, fruits, and local specialties.

Why Choose It: Hotel Carlton is perfect for those who want a budget-friendly stay in the heart of the city, with easy access to tourist attractions and a comfortable, no-frills experience.

Hotel Tiba

Located in the city center, Hotel Tiba offers a cozy and affordable stay for travelers on a budget. With simple yet comfortable accommodations, it's a good choice for visitors who want to experience Tunis without spending too much.

Key Features:

- **Budget-Friendly**: Hotel Tiba offers some of the most affordable rates in the city, making it a great option for budget-conscious travelers.
- **Comfortable Rooms**: Rooms are equipped with basic amenities, including air conditioning, free Wi-Fi, and TV. While the rooms are simple, they offer everything you need for a comfortable stay.
- **Central Location**: Situated close to Tunis' main attractions, including the Medina and the National Theatre, Hotel Tiba is a great choice for those wanting to explore the city without a long commute.
- **On-Site Dining**: The hotel's small restaurant offers a range of Tunisian dishes and international options, perfect for those who don't want to venture far for a meal.

Why Choose It: Hotel Tiba is ideal for travelers looking for an affordable yet comfortable stay with a central location and all the basic amenities needed for a pleasant trip.

Hotel Tunisia Palace

Situated near Tunis' main shopping areas, Hotel Tunisia Palace offers great value for money in a central location. The hotel combines classic elegance with modern comforts, making it a solid mid-range option for travelers who want an easygoing, comfortable stay.

Key Features:

- **Classic Design**: The hotel's interiors feature traditional Tunisian design elements, including tilework and classic furnishings, creating a charming atmosphere for guests.
- **Convenient Location**: Located within walking distance of many of the city's most famous attractions, including the Medina and the Bardo Museum, Hotel Tunisia Palace offers easy access to culture, shopping, and dining.
- **Reasonable Rates**: Offering competitive prices for the area, this hotel provides an excellent balance of value and comfort.
- **Amenities**: The hotel offers comfortable rooms, free Wi-Fi, a small business center, and a pleasant lounge area for relaxation.

Why Choose It: Hotel Tunisia Palace is perfect for those looking for an elegant and affordable stay with a central location and easy access to Tunis' attractions.

Hostels and Guesthouses in Tunis

For travelers looking for social, budget-friendly accommodations, hostels and guesthouses in Tunis are a great choice. These types of lodging offer affordable prices, a more relaxed atmosphere, and an opportunity to meet fellow travelers. With their laid-back vibe and often central locations, hostels and guesthouses are ideal for young backpackers, solo travelers, or anyone looking to explore Tunis without spending a lot on accommodation. Here are some of the top hostels and guesthouses in Tunis that combine affordability with a warm, welcoming environment.

The Medina Hostel

The Medina Hostel is a popular choice for backpackers and solo travelers seeking an affordable, social, and centrally located place to stay. It offers a perfect blend of comfort, community, and convenience, located right in the heart of the historical Medina.

Key Features:

- **Prime Location**: The Medina Hostel is located just steps away from the bustling souks and historical sites like the Zitouna Mosque and Bardo Museum, making it an ideal base for exploring Tunis.
- **Community Atmosphere**: The hostel's common areas are designed to encourage interaction among travelers. The cozy lounge is perfect for socializing, while the outdoor courtyard provides a relaxed setting for guests to unwind and chat.
- **Affordable Rates**: As one of the more budget-friendly options in the city, The Medina Hostel offers dormitory beds as well as private rooms, providing flexibility for different types of travelers.
- **Free Wi-Fi and Kitchen**: The hostel provides free Wi-Fi, allowing guests to stay connected, and a shared kitchen for those who want to prepare their own meals.

Why Choose It: The Medina Hostel is ideal for travelers who want to stay in a social, budget-friendly environment. With its central location and community-focused atmosphere, it's a great place for solo travelers or those looking to meet people while exploring Tunis.

Tunis Youth Hostel

The Tunis Youth Hostel, run by the Tunisian Youth Hostels Federation, is an excellent choice for young travelers or those on a tight budget. It offers clean, simple accommodations with a focus on comfort and affordability.

Key Features:

- **Affordable and Basic Rooms**: Offering dormitory-style rooms and private options, the Tunis Youth Hostel provides clean, basic accommodations perfect for budget travelers.
- **Convenient Location**: Located near the city center, guests can easily explore Tunis' major attractions, including the Medina, National Museum of Carthage, and the vibrant Habib Bourguiba Avenue.
- **Friendly Atmosphere**: The hostel staff are friendly and welcoming, often providing useful travel tips and helping guests with local transportation options or directions to nearby attractions.
- **Shared Kitchen and Lounge**: There is a shared kitchen where guests can prepare their own meals, and a common lounge area for relaxing and socializing.

Why Choose It: The Tunis Youth Hostel is a great option for young travelers or anyone looking for a simple, no-frills place to stay while keeping costs low. It's a good choice for those seeking a clean, friendly, and social environment.

Dar El Jeld

Dar El Jeld is a charming guesthouse located in the Medina, offering an intimate, homely atmosphere combined with affordable rates. It's a great option for those who prefer a quieter, more personal experience compared to larger hostels.

Key Features:

- **Traditional Tunisian Architecture**: Dar El Jeld is housed in a beautifully restored historical building that combines traditional Tunisian style with modern comforts.
- **Cultural Experience**: Guests can enjoy the authentic Tunisian décor and local hospitality, making this guesthouse an excellent way to immerse yourself in the culture of Tunis.
- **Personalized Service**: The owners and staff are friendly and knowledgeable, often going the extra mile to ensure a comfortable stay and provide recommendations for local attractions and activities.
- **Peaceful and Relaxed**: Unlike large hostels, Dar El Jeld offers a more intimate and tranquil environment, with just a few rooms available. It's a great choice for those seeking a peaceful retreat after a day of exploring the city.

Why Choose It: Perfect for travelers who are looking for a more personalized, quiet stay while still being able to experience the cultural richness of Tunis. Dar El Jeld offers an intimate and affordable option for those who value comfort and local charm.

La Maison Blanche

La Maison Blanche is a guesthouse that blends modern comforts with a traditional Tunisian style, offering an excellent option for those seeking a quiet retreat with easy access to the city. It's located just outside the busy Medina, providing a peaceful escape with a short commute to key sites.

Key Features:

- **Modern yet Traditional**: La Maison Blanche features a blend of contemporary design and traditional Tunisian elements, creating a cozy and welcoming atmosphere for guests.
- **Quiet Location**: The guesthouse is situated in a quieter neighborhood, providing a peaceful atmosphere while still being a short walk or drive from the city's major attractions.
- **Homely Feel**: With just a few rooms available, La Maison Blanche offers a more personal and homely experience. The staff are friendly and helpful, providing a more intimate level of service.
- **Terrace and Garden**: The guesthouse has a charming terrace and garden, perfect for relaxing with a cup of tea or enjoying the Tunisian sun.

Why Choose It: For travelers looking for a quieter, more personalized experience in Tunis, La Maison Blanche offers a comfortable and affordable option with easy access to the city's attractions.

Hostel El Medina

Located in the heart of Tunis, Hostel El Medina offers a vibrant, social environment where guests can meet fellow travelers while enjoying comfortable, affordable accommodations. It's a great place for those who want to experience the energy of the Medina while staying on a budget.

Key Features:

- **Central Location**: Just a short walk from the Medina and Avenue Habib Bourguiba, Hostel El Medina is perfectly located for travelers wanting to explore the historic heart of Tunis.
- **Dormitory and Private Rooms**: The hostel offers both dormitory-style and private rooms, making it a versatile option for different types of travelers.
- **Social Environment**: The hostel is known for its friendly, social atmosphere, with common areas where guests can relax, swap travel stories, and plan their next adventure.
- **Free Wi-Fi and Breakfast**: Hostel El Medina provides free Wi-Fi and a simple continental breakfast, making it easy to start the day and stay connected with friends or family.

Why Choose It: Hostel El Medina is perfect for travelers who want a social, budget-friendly place to stay with easy access to the city's major attractions. It's a good option for solo travelers or groups looking to meet new people.

Riads in Tunis

Riads, traditional Tunisian homes transformed into guesthouses, offer a unique and immersive lodging experience for travelers seeking authenticity, charm, and a deep connection to the local culture. These accommodations are typically situated within the winding streets of the Medina, offering an intimate and culturally rich environment. Riads in Tunis combine the elegance of traditional architecture with modern amenities, providing a peaceful retreat in the heart of the city. Here are some of the top picks for riads in Tunis, where you can experience the warmth of Tunisian hospitality and the beauty of traditional living.

Dar Ben Gacem

Dar Ben Gacem is a beautifully restored 18th-century riad located in the historic Medina of Tunis. It offers a charming blend of traditional Tunisian architecture with modern comforts, making it an ideal spot for travelers seeking a peaceful, culturally immersive stay.

Key Features:

- **Authentic Atmosphere**: The riad's interior is decorated with traditional Tunisian tiles, intricate woodwork, and elegant furnishings that reflect the rich heritage of Tunis.
- **Personalized Service**: The owners and staff are friendly and attentive, offering personalized recommendations for local attractions and experiences in the Medina.
- **Peaceful Courtyard**: The riad features a stunning central courtyard with lush greenery, providing a quiet oasis in the middle of the bustling city.
- **Comfortable Rooms**: Rooms are spacious, with air conditioning, free Wi-Fi, and beautiful traditional décor. Some rooms also feature views over the Medina.

- **Location**: Situated just a short walk from the main attractions of the Medina, such as the Zitouna Mosque and the souks, Dar Ben Gacem is ideally located for exploring the cultural heart of Tunis.

Why Choose It: For travelers looking for an authentic experience in a beautifully restored traditional home, Dar Ben Gacem offers the perfect balance of cultural immersion, comfort, and modern amenities.

Dar El Médina

Located in the heart of the Medina, Dar El Médina is a traditional riad that has been meticulously renovated to offer a luxurious and comfortable stay. The riad captures the essence of Tunisian hospitality with its beautiful interiors, serene ambiance, and exceptional service.

Key Features:

- **Elegant Design**: The riad is known for its stunning traditional Tunisian architecture, featuring intricately designed wooden doors, colorful tiles, and high ceilings that evoke a sense of historical grandeur.
- **Private Courtyard**: Guests can relax in the peaceful courtyard surrounded by flowering plants, offering an ideal space to unwind after a day of sightseeing.
- **Cultural Experience**: The riad offers guests a chance to experience Tunisian life up close, with its authentic décor and proximity to the local souks and markets.
- **Comfortable Rooms**: Rooms at Dar El Médina are tastefully decorated with local textiles and art, and

equipped with modern amenities such as air conditioning, en-suite bathrooms, and free Wi-Fi.
- **Personalized Attention**: The staff at Dar El Médina is known for their warm hospitality, offering tailored recommendations and ensuring that guests feel at home.

Why Choose It: Dar El Médina is perfect for travelers seeking a luxurious yet authentic experience in the heart of Tunis' historic district. The riad's beautiful design, peaceful atmosphere, and central location make it an ideal choice for a relaxing stay.

Dar Ya

Dar Ya is an intimate and cozy riad nestled in the Medina of Tunis, offering a truly traditional experience with a focus on comfort and local authenticity. It provides an excellent base for those wishing to explore the city's cultural and historical gems.

Key Features:

- **Charming Traditional Decor**: Dar Ya's décor showcases authentic Tunisian art, colorful carpets, and handcrafted furniture that give the space a warm and welcoming atmosphere.
- **Homely Feel**: With only a few rooms available, Dar Ya provides a more personalized and intimate stay. The riad's small size ensures that guests receive attention and care from the hosts.
- **Comfort and Relaxation**: The riad features a beautiful rooftop terrace where guests can relax and enjoy views of the Medina and beyond. The rooms are simple yet comfortable, with traditional touches and modern amenities.

- **Central Location**: Situated in the heart of the Medina, Dar Ya is just a short walk from key landmarks such as the Zitouna Mosque and the local souks, offering guests an excellent opportunity to experience Tunisian culture firsthand.
- **Traditional Breakfast**: Guests can enjoy a delicious Tunisian breakfast served in the riad's intimate dining area, offering fresh bread, olives, cheese, and traditional pastries.

Why Choose It: Dar Ya is perfect for travelers looking for a peaceful, intimate, and culturally immersive experience. The small scale of the riad and its traditional setting create a welcoming atmosphere that makes guests feel like part of a family.

Dar Sidi Saïd

Dar Sidi Saïd is a luxurious riad located near the famous Sidi Bou Said area, offering a tranquil environment with spectacular views of the Mediterranean. This riad combines traditional Tunisian charm with modern amenities, making it a perfect choice for those seeking both relaxation and cultural exploration.

Key Features:

- **Breathtaking Views**: Located just outside the Medina, Dar Sidi Saïd offers stunning views of the Mediterranean Sea, providing a peaceful and serene atmosphere for guests.
- **Tunisian Heritage**: The riad is decorated with traditional Tunisian craftsmanship, including vibrant tile work, rich

wood finishes, and detailed carvings, giving it a luxurious yet authentic feel.
- **Peaceful Retreat**: Guests can unwind in the beautiful courtyards or enjoy the panoramic views from the riad's terrace.
- **Exclusive Rooms**: Each room is individually decorated, with a blend of traditional Tunisian style and modern comfort. Rooms feature air conditioning, free Wi-Fi, and en-suite bathrooms.
- **Ideal Location**: The riad is just a short drive from the picturesque village of Sidi Bou Said, famous for its blue and white architecture, and close to key cultural attractions in Tunis.

Why Choose It: For those seeking a luxurious riad experience with views of the Mediterranean, Dar Sidi Saïd provides an ideal blend of relaxation, cultural immersion, and comfort.

Dar Zitouna

Dar Zitouna offers a charming, traditional riad experience in the heart of the Medina, just steps from the famous Zitouna Mosque. This small guesthouse offers a perfect blend of comfort, authenticity, and a homely atmosphere.

Key Features:

- **Authentic and Cozy**: The riad's traditional design includes mosaic-tiled floors, high wooden beams, and colorful textiles, creating an inviting and cozy atmosphere.

- **Personalized Service**: With a small number of rooms, the staff at Dar Zitouna are able to offer personalized service, ensuring that each guest has a memorable experience.
- **Great Location**: Located near the heart of the Medina, Dar Zitouna is within walking distance of many of Tunis' top attractions, including the souks, historic sites, and local eateries.
- **Traditional Ambiance**: Guests can enjoy traditional Tunisian breakfast and meals served in the riad's cozy dining area, with a focus on fresh, local ingredients.
- **Comfortable Rooms**: The rooms at Dar Zitouna are equipped with modern amenities, such as air conditioning and free Wi-Fi, while maintaining a traditional aesthetic.

Why Choose It: Dar Zitouna offers an intimate, authentic experience in a beautifully restored riad, perfect for those seeking a personal and culturally immersive stay in the Medina.

Essential Tips for Booking Accommodations in Tunis

1. **Book in Advance**: Especially during peak tourist seasons (spring and summer), accommodations in Tunis can fill up quickly. It's advisable to book your stay well in advance to secure the best options and rates.
2. **Consider Location**: Choose your accommodation based on proximity to key attractions or neighborhoods that suit your preferences. The Medina offers a historical experience, while areas like La Marsa and Carthage are ideal for coastal views.
3. **Know Your Budget**: Tunis offers a wide range of accommodations, from luxury hotels to budget-friendly

hostels. Set a clear budget and look for options that meet both your financial and comfort needs.

4. **Check Amenities**: Ensure the accommodation offers the necessary amenities like Wi-Fi, air conditioning (important in summer), free parking, and breakfast, depending on your needs.
5. **Read Reviews**: Always check reviews from other travelers on trusted platforms like TripAdvisor or Booking.com. They can provide valuable insights about cleanliness, service quality, and overall experience.
6. **Payment and Cancellation Policies**: Understand the payment terms (e.g., deposit, full payment) and cancellation policy. Some places offer more flexible options, while others may require a non-refundable deposit.
7. **Consider Length of Stay**: For longer stays, serviced apartments or vacation rentals may offer better value, providing the flexibility of cooking and more space for relaxation.
8. **Look for Local Experiences**: If you're looking for something unique, consider staying in a riad or boutique hotel that reflects Tunisian culture, offering an authentic local experience.
9. **Check Transport Options**: Consider how accessible the accommodation is from key transport hubs (train stations, airport) and whether public transport or taxis are easily available.
10. **Confirm Special Requests**: If you have any special needs, such as accessibility requirements or early check-in, contact the accommodation directly to confirm they can accommodate your requests.

Useful Websites and Resources for Booking Accommodations in Tunis

1. **Booking.com**
   - **Why It's Useful**: One of the most popular global platforms for booking accommodations. Offers a wide range of options from luxury hotels to budget hostels and serviced apartments. It also provides guest reviews, detailed descriptions, and free cancellation options for many properties.
   - **Website**: Booking.com
2. **Airbnb**
   - **Why It's Useful**: Ideal for those looking for unique stays such as vacation rentals, riads, or local homes. Airbnb offers the flexibility of self-catering with the option to book experiences or guided tours with locals.
   - **Website**: Airbnb
3. **Expedia**
   - **Why It's Useful**: Expedia allows you to compare prices for hotels, vacation rentals, and even flights and car rentals, making it a great resource for organizing an entire trip. Their user-friendly interface and package deals can help you save on multiple bookings.
   - **Website**: Expedia
4. **TripAdvisor**
   - **Why It's Useful**: Provides comprehensive reviews and ratings of hotels, vacation rentals, and other accommodations. It's an excellent resource for

checking traveler feedback before making a reservation.
  - **Website**: TripAdvisor
5. **Hotels.com**
   - **Why It's Useful**: Known for its loyalty program that gives you a free night after booking ten nights. Hotels.com offers a broad selection of properties across different price ranges and often features promotions and discounts.
   - **Website**: Hotels.com
6. **Trivago**
   - **Why It's Useful**: Trivago compares prices across multiple hotel booking websites, helping you find the best deals and offers for your stay. It includes options for luxury hotels, boutique stays, and budget accommodations.
   - **Website**: Trivago
7. **Agoda**
   - **Why It's Useful**: While originally focused on Asia, Agoda has expanded its offerings globally and is known for competitive prices, especially for hotels and serviced apartments. Their loyalty program can help you earn rewards.
   - **Website**: Agoda
8. **Zarzis (Local Tunisian Platform)**
   - **Why It's Useful**: This is a local Tunisian platform for booking hotels, guesthouses, and apartments across the country. It's a great resource for finding accommodations that reflect local hospitality and charm.
   - **Website**: Zarzis

9. **Tunisian Tourism Office (ONTT)**
    - **Why It's Useful**: For authentic and detailed information on accommodations throughout Tunisia, the official Tunisian tourism website provides a list of certified hotels, vacation homes, and more, along with local travel guides and event information.
    - **Website**: ONTT
10. **Hostelworld**
    - **Why It's Useful**: Best for budget travelers and backpackers looking for hostels or shared accommodations in Tunis. Hostelworld offers detailed reviews, ratings, and booking options for affordable stays.
    - **Website**: Hostelworld
11. **Tripping.com**
    - **Why It's Useful**: A meta-search engine that compares vacation rental prices from sites like Airbnb, Booking.com, and others. It's perfect for finding unique rental properties in Tunis.
    - **Website**: Tripping.com

Conclusion on Accommodation Options in Tunis

Tunis offers a wide variety of accommodation options to suit every type of traveler, from luxurious hotels and boutique stays to affordable hostels and unique riads. Whether you're looking for a lavish experience with top-tier amenities, a charming and intimate environment in a boutique hotel, or the flexibility and comfort of serviced apartments, the city has something to meet your needs. For budget-conscious travelers, there are plenty of affordable options, including hostels, guesthouses, and vacation rentals. By considering factors like location, budget, and preferred amenities, travelers can easily find the perfect accommodation to enhance their Tunisian experience.

TOP ATTRACTIONS IN TUNIS

Tunis top attractions offer a captivating mix of ancient ruins, religious landmarks, and stunning architectural marvels. From the historic Medina to the breathtaking Zitouna Mosque and the lively Habib Bourguiba Avenue, Tunis is home to numerous sites that reflect the country's diverse heritage. If you're drawn to the grandeur of colonial-era buildings, the tranquility of traditional gardens, or the fascinating museums that preserve the city's history, Tunis promises an unforgettable experience for all types of travelers.

The Medina of Tunis

The Medina of Tunis is one of the most iconic and historical neighborhoods in the capital city of Tunisia. As a UNESCO World Heritage site, the Medina is the heart of the city, offering a captivating journey through narrow, winding alleyways, bustling souks, and ancient Islamic architecture. It's a must-see destination for anyone visiting Tunis.

Historical Significance

- The Medina dates back to the 7th century and represents the classical example of a traditional Arab-Islamic city. It was originally built to accommodate both the religious and commercial needs of the city, with mosques, palaces, and markets scattered across its labyrinth of streets.
- Over time, the Medina evolved into the political and cultural center of Tunis. It is home to numerous

monuments, such as the **Zitouna Mosque**, which remains a key place of worship and an important symbol of Tunisian Islam.

Main Attractions

1. **Zitouna Mosque:**
   - This mosque is the largest and most significant in the Medina, serving as the center of religious life. It was founded in the 8th century and is renowned for its beautiful architecture, including ornate arches, an impressive minaret, and a peaceful courtyard.
   - **Tip:** Non-Muslim visitors can only visit the exterior and the courtyard.
2. **Souk el-Attarine (Perfume Market):**
   - One of the most aromatic markets in the Medina, Souk el-Attarine offers a variety of perfumes, oils, and traditional remedies. Visitors can also find a wide range of spices and incense. The vibrant colors and intoxicating scents make it a fantastic sensory experience.
   - **Tip:** Don't hesitate to haggle with the vendors to get the best price on your perfume or spice purchases.
3. **Souk des Chechias (Traditional Hat Market):**
   - A famous market in the Medina where you can find the traditional **chechia**, a red woolen cap that is an iconic symbol of Tunisia. The market offers a fascinating display of craftsmanship and is a great place to purchase local handmade souvenirs.

- Tip: This is a perfect place for unique, authentic gifts. Be sure to ask the shopkeepers about the history of the chechia and its cultural significance.

4. **Dar Hussein Palace:**
    - This former royal palace is now a cultural museum. The palace is a prime example of 18th-century Tunisian architecture and design, showcasing intricate wooden carvings, decorative tiles, and luxurious rooms. The palace offers insight into Tunisia's opulent past.
    - Tip: Visit in the morning when it's quieter to explore the ornate rooms and take photographs.
5. **Place du Gouvernement (Government Square):**
    - This central square is surrounded by significant historical buildings and offers a look into Tunisia's political history. It's a perfect place to sit and enjoy the atmosphere of the Medina.
    - Tip: The square is often busy, so take some time to relax in a café nearby and watch the world go by.

Practical Tips for Visiting the Medina of Tunis

- **Getting There:** The Medina is easily accessible by taxi, bus, or walking from central Tunis. If you're coming by public transport, you can get off at **Bab el-Bahr**, the main entrance to the Medina.
- **Navigating the Medina:** The Medina's streets can be a maze, so it's recommended to bring a map or hire a local guide to help you navigate the maze of alleyways.
- **Best Time to Visit:** Early mornings or late afternoons are ideal times to explore the Medina to avoid the crowds and

heat. It also offers a more authentic experience, as the souks and streets are less busy.
- **Safety Tips:** While the Medina is a relatively safe place to visit, it's always important to watch out for pickpockets, especially in crowded areas. Keep your belongings secure and avoid carrying large sums of cash.

Carthage Archaeological Site

Carthage, an ancient city located on the coast of Tunisia, was once the center of a powerful empire that rivaled Rome. The **Carthage Archaeological Site** today is one of the most important and well-preserved sites in the Mediterranean, offering visitors a chance to explore its rich history and incredible ruins.

Historical Significance

- Founded by the Phoenicians in the 9th century BCE, Carthage became one of the most influential cities in the ancient world, known for its maritime dominance, wealth, and cultural achievements. The city reached its peak under the leadership of Queen Dido and later, during the Punic Wars, was at the center of fierce conflicts with Rome.
- The city was famously destroyed by the Romans in 146 BCE during the Third Punic War but was later rebuilt under Roman rule. Today, visitors can explore the layers of history embedded in the archaeological ruins of the ancient city.

Main Attractions

1. **Antonine Baths:**

- The Antonine Baths are among the largest and best-preserved Roman bath complexes in the world. Built in the 2nd century CE, the baths were an important social and cultural hub for Carthage's citizens. The site consists of expansive courtyards, grand arches, and massive rooms that would have once been filled with warm water.
- **Tip:** Take your time to explore the site and imagine the grandeur of this bathhouse. The views of the Mediterranean from the site are stunning.

2. **Byrsa Hill:**
    - Byrsa Hill was the heart of Carthage, home to the city's royal palace and important religious sites. The hill offers panoramic views of the Mediterranean and Tunis, making it a great spot for photography.
    - **Tip:** Don't miss the Carthage Museum located on Byrsa Hill, which showcases artifacts found throughout the site, including sculptures, mosaics, and pottery.
3. **Tophet Cemetery:**
    - The Tophet Cemetery is an ancient burial ground believed to be used for the sacrifice of children in the Phoenician and Carthaginian religious practices. The site contains thousands of urns containing the remains of infants and young children.
    - **Tip:** Approach the site with sensitivity, as it is a solemn and historical place. It offers a glimpse into the religious practices of the Carthaginians.
4. **Roman Villas:**
    - The Roman Villas in Carthage are sprawling homes that showcase Roman architectural prowess. These

villas were decorated with beautiful mosaics and walls adorned with frescoes, depicting scenes from daily life and Roman mythology.
- **Tip:** Take a guided tour to learn more about the significance of these homes and the people who lived there.

5. **Punic Ports:**
   - Carthage's Punic Ports, one of the largest and most advanced ports of the ancient world, were crucial to the city's commercial success. The site offers fascinating insights into the naval power of the Carthaginians.
   - **Tip:** The Punic Ports are best explored with a guide who can explain the naval history of Carthage.

Practical Tips for Visiting the Carthage Archaeological Site

- **Getting There:** The Carthage Archaeological Site is easily accessible from Tunis by taxi or train. The **Carthage - Byrsa** train station is located near the site, making it a convenient stop.
- **Best Time to Visit:** The site is best visited early in the morning or late afternoon, particularly during the warmer months when the Mediterranean sun can be intense. Avoid midday visits during summer.
- **Admission Fees:** There is an entrance fee for the various sites in Carthage, and it's possible to purchase a combined ticket that covers multiple sites, such as the Antonine Baths, Byrsa Hill, and the Roman Villas.
- **Guided Tours:** Hiring a local guide is recommended for a more comprehensive understanding of the history and

significance of the site. Many of the ruins can be difficult to interpret without historical context.

Sidi Bou Said

Sidi Bou Said is one of the most picturesque and enchanting towns in Tunisia, known for its striking blue-and-white color scheme, cobbled streets, and breathtaking views over the Mediterranean Sea. Situated just a short drive from Tunis, this charming village is often described as a "living postcard" due to its beauty and serene atmosphere.

Historical Significance

- Sidi Bou Said has been a center for artists, intellectuals, and the upper class throughout history, attracting a diverse range of visitors from across Tunisia and beyond. The village is named after **Sidi Bou Said**, a 13th-century religious scholar and saint, who is said to have lived in the area. His tomb, located near the village's entrance, remains a focal point of spiritual significance.
- The town's unique architectural style — with its whitewashed buildings, blue shutters, and tiled roofs — was influenced by a combination of Ottoman, Andalusian, and Berber traditions. This distinctive aesthetic has become synonymous with the town's identity and is a key draw for visitors today.

Main Attractions

1. **Ennejma Ezzahra Palace:**
    - Also known as the **Palace of the Star of Zahra**, this beautifully restored palace dates back to the

early 20th century and is a prime example of traditional Tunisian architecture. It was once the residence of Baron Rodolphe d'Erlanger, a French aristocrat and musicologist who fell in love with the region's history and culture. Today, it serves as a museum dedicated to the arts, including music, sculpture, and fine craftsmanship.
    - **Tip:** Take a guided tour to learn about the palace's history and its connection to the cultural revival of Sidi Bou Said. The museum's collection of art, especially the intricate Arabic calligraphy, is well worth exploring.
2. **The Blue-and-White Architecture:**
    - Walking through Sidi Bou Said feels like stepping into a different world, with its trademark blue and white color scheme. The whitewashed walls of the houses provide a bright contrast to the striking blue shutters, doors, and window frames, which were inspired by the vibrant hues of the Mediterranean. The town's architecture is designed to harmonize with its coastal surroundings, blending seamlessly into the landscape.
    - **Tip:** Sidi Bou Said is best explored on foot to fully appreciate its narrow, winding streets and the views of the surrounding area. Make sure to take a stroll down to the sea and enjoy the stunning vistas.
3. **Café des Délices:**
    - Located on a hill with an unparalleled view of the Mediterranean Sea, Café des Délices is an iconic spot in Sidi Bou Said. This café is a popular hangout for both locals and tourists, offering

refreshing mint tea and traditional Tunisian pastries. The café's reputation has also been immortalized in the famous French film **"The Sheltering Sky"** by Bernardo Bertolucci, in which it served as a backdrop.
- o **Tip:** Visit around sunset for an unforgettable view of the sea as the sun dips below the horizon. Don't forget to try a traditional **Makroud**, a sweet semolina cake filled with dates or nuts.

4. **The Tomb of Sidi Bou Said:**
   - o The tomb of Sidi Bou Said, the town's namesake, is located near the entrance to the village. The tomb is a simple yet serene site and draws both pilgrims and visitors seeking a moment of tranquility. The site is also an important landmark for local Muslims and holds historical and religious significance.
   - o **Tip:** Respect the local customs and dress modestly when visiting the tomb. Take a moment to reflect in this peaceful spot, where the atmosphere of devotion and spirituality is palpable.

5. **Sidi Bou Said's Art Galleries:**
   - o Over the years, Sidi Bou Said has become a hub for artists, with numerous galleries and workshops scattered throughout the village. The combination of stunning natural beauty, calm atmosphere, and rich history has made the town a haven for painters, sculptors, and photographers. Many of the galleries showcase local art, offering a glimpse into the country's creative spirit.
   - o **Tip:** Visit one of the art galleries to discover works by local Tunisian artists, ranging from

contemporary paintings to traditional crafts. Consider purchasing a unique piece of art as a souvenir.

Practical Tips for Visiting Sidi Bou Said

- **Getting There:** Sidi Bou Said is a short 20-minute drive from Tunis, or you can take the TGM (Tunis-Goulette-Marsa) train from Tunis to the **Sidi Bou Said** station. The train ride offers scenic views along the coast and is a convenient and affordable way to reach the village.
- **Best Time to Visit:** Spring and fall are the best times to visit, as the weather is mild and pleasant. Summer months can be very hot, and the town can get crowded with tourists.
- **Dress Code:** Sidi Bou Said is a conservative town, so it's advisable to dress modestly, especially when visiting religious sites like the tomb. Lightweight, breathable clothing is recommended for the warm climate.
- **Safety Tips:** Sidi Bou Said is a safe and friendly place for tourists, but like any popular destination, it's important to be mindful of your belongings, especially in crowded areas.

The Bardo National Museum

The **Bardo National Museum** is one of the most significant museums in Africa and is considered the treasure trove of Tunisia's rich and diverse history. Located in the heart of Tunis, the museum is housed in a former palace that combines grand architecture with an extensive collection of archaeological artifacts.

Historical Significance

- The Bardo Museum's origins date back to the 19th century when it was originally the residence of the Husainid dynasty, which ruled Tunisia from the 18th to the 20th century. The palace itself is a stunning example of Islamic architecture, with beautiful courtyards, ornate ceilings, and intricate tile work.
- The museum's collection spans thousands of years, offering a deep dive into Tunisia's ancient history, from the **Punic** era through the **Roman**, **Byzantine**, and **Islamic** periods. The museum is especially renowned for its vast collection of **Roman mosaics**, which are considered some of the finest in the world.

Main Attractions

1. **Roman Mosaics:**
   - The Bardo Museum is home to the world's largest collection of Roman mosaics, many of which were excavated from sites across Tunisia, including Carthage and Dougga. These mosaics depict scenes of everyday Roman life, mythology, and Roman gods and goddesses, often with intricate detail and vibrant colors.
   - **Tip:** Allow time to truly appreciate the scale and detail of the mosaics. Some of the most famous mosaics include the **Punic Ship Mosaic** and the **The Four Seasons Mosaic**.
2. **Punic Artifacts:**
   - The museum also holds a remarkable collection of **Punic** artifacts, offering insight into the life of the

Carthaginian civilization. This includes items such as **ceramics**, **jewelry**, and **sculptures**, which provide a glimpse into the daily lives and religious practices of the Carthaginians.
  - **Tip:** Don't miss the **Tophet Cemetery Urns**, which offer a sobering insight into the ancient religious practices involving child sacrifices.
3. **Byzantine and Islamic Collections:**
   - In addition to the Roman and Punic collections, the Bardo Museum houses an impressive array of **Byzantine** and **Islamic** artifacts, including textiles, coins, and ceramics. The Islamic section of the museum highlights Tunisia's cultural and artistic achievements during the Islamic period.
   - **Tip:** The **Islamic Art** section of the museum is a quiet, peaceful space with beautiful calligraphy and intricate designs, offering visitors a chance to reflect on the Islamic influence in Tunisia.
4. **The Carthage Room:**
   - This room is dedicated to the ancient city of **Carthage** and displays a variety of **Carthaginian** treasures, including sculptures, pottery, and inscriptions. The room provides a deeper understanding of the history and culture of the Carthaginians, as well as their eventual downfall at the hands of the Romans.
   - **Tip:** This section is particularly insightful for those interested in the **Punic Wars** and the historical rivalry between Carthage and Rome.
5. **The Mummy Room:**

- The Bardo Museum also has a fascinating **mummy collection**, showcasing the ancient Egyptian influence on Tunisia. The mummies on display are part of the museum's extensive archaeological collections, some of which were discovered in Tunisia and date back thousands of years.
- **Tip:** The mummies and the artifacts associated with them offer a rare glimpse into the Egyptian presence in North Africa, making this room a unique stop within the museum.

Practical Tips for Visiting the Bardo National Museum

- **Getting There:** The Bardo Museum is easily accessible by taxi, bus, or train from central Tunis. It's about a 10-minute drive from the city center.
- **Best Time to Visit:** The museum is often less crowded on weekdays, making it a great time to visit if you prefer a quieter experience. Arrive early to avoid large groups.
- **Admission Fees:** The entrance fee to the museum is very reasonable, with discounts available for students and groups.
- **Guided Tours:** Consider hiring a guide or renting an audio guide to get the most out of your visit. The museum's vast collection can be overwhelming, and a guide can provide historical context and interesting anecdotes.

Zitouna Mosque

The Zitouna Mosque, also known as the Great Mosque of Tunis, is a symbol of the city's Islamic heritage and one of the most important religious landmarks in Tunisia. It is located in the heart of the Medina, the historic walled center of Tunis, and dates back to 732 AD, making it one of the oldest and most significant mosques in North Africa.

Key Features and Highlights:

1. **Architectural Marvel**:
   - The mosque is a blend of various architectural styles, including the classical Islamic, Andalusian, and Fatimid influences. It features a large rectangular prayer hall, with beautiful marble columns, intricate arches, and decorative stucco work.
   - The mosque's **minaret** stands out against the Tunis skyline. It is 44 meters high and is one of the most iconic features of the mosque.
   - The **inner courtyard** is spacious, featuring a serene fountain at its center, surrounded by lush greenery and arcades that provide shade to visitors.
2. **Rich History**:
   - Zitouna Mosque has served as a key religious, educational, and political center throughout Tunisian history. It was initially built as a place of worship, but over time, it also became a prestigious center of learning, attracting scholars from across the Muslim world.
   - The mosque's **library** was historically one of the most important in the region, housing many manuscripts and religious texts. Some of these texts are still preserved in various institutions today.

3. **Interior Design**:
   - Inside, the mosque is renowned for its **ornate decoration**, including intricately carved wooden doors, ornate marble floors, and beautiful ceramic tile work. The prayer hall is vast, with a grand mihrab (prayer niche) and a **mimber** (pulpit) made of finely carved wood.
   - The **maqsura**, a special area reserved for the ruling elite, is elegantly decorated with wood carvings and colorful tiles. This is a testament to the mosque's historic importance as a space not only for worship but also for governance.

Visitor Tips:

- **Dress Modestly**: As a place of active worship, visitors should dress modestly when entering the mosque. Women should cover their heads with a scarf, and men should avoid wearing shorts or sleeveless shirts.
- **Visiting Hours**: The mosque is open to visitors outside of prayer times. However, it is advisable to check the prayer schedule before visiting to ensure you are not interrupting religious services.
- **Respect Local Customs**: While tourists are allowed to visit, they should be mindful of the mosque's sacred atmosphere. Visitors should speak quietly and avoid disruptive behavior.
- **Nearby Attractions**: The mosque is located near many other historic sites within the Medina, so it's a great starting point for a tour of the old city, including the nearby souks (markets) and the Dar Hussein Palace.

Belvedere Park

Belvedere Park (Parc du Belvédère) is a lush and expansive green space in Tunis that offers both locals and visitors a welcome retreat from the bustle of the city. Situated on a hilltop, the park provides stunning views over Tunis, the nearby Gulf of Tunis, and the surrounding landscape.

Key Features and Highlights:

1. **Scenic Views**:
   - Located on a hill, Belvedere Park offers one of the best panoramic views in the city. From here, you can see the coastline of Tunis and the urban sprawl of the capital. It's especially beautiful during sunset, when the city is bathed in golden light.
   - The park is also home to a **small lake**, adding to its tranquil atmosphere. Many locals come here to relax by the water or take leisurely strolls through the park's paths.
2. **Belvedere Zoo**:
   - Within the park, you'll find the **Belvedere Zoo**, one of the oldest zoos in Tunisia. It houses a variety of animals, including species native to Tunisia as well as exotic animals from other parts of the world. The zoo is family-friendly, and children can enjoy seeing animals like monkeys, lions, and various bird species.

- The zoo is well-maintained, and the green space around it makes for a pleasant environment to spend a few hours.
3. **Museum of Modern Art**:
    - The park also hosts the **Museum of Modern Art** (Musée d'Art Moderne), which is located within a beautiful colonial-era building. The museum displays a variety of contemporary Tunisian art, including paintings, sculptures, and installations by both emerging and established artists.
    - The museum offers a cultural contrast to the park's natural beauty, allowing visitors to immerse themselves in Tunisia's modern artistic scene while enjoying the park's serene environment.
4. **Recreational Facilities**:
    - Belvedere Park is perfect for picnics, leisurely walks, or simply relaxing in the shade of its trees. It has several benches and open lawns where visitors can sit and enjoy the outdoors.
    - There are also well-maintained walking and jogging paths, making it a popular spot for morning exercise. Fitness enthusiasts and joggers come here to start their day with a refreshing run through the park.
5. **Family-Friendly Atmosphere**:
    - With its wide-open spaces and numerous playgrounds, Belvedere Park is an excellent destination for families. Children can play in the designated areas, and there are often local events or activities for kids during weekends and holidays.

- o The park is safe, clean, and well-patrolled, making it a popular destination for both locals and tourists, especially during the weekends.

Visitor Tips:

- **Best Time to Visit**: The park is open year-round, but the best time to visit is during the spring or autumn months when the weather is mild and pleasant. Avoid the summer heat, as it can get quite hot in Tunis.
- **Entry Fee**: There is a small entry fee to access the zoo, but the park itself is free to enter. The museum may also charge an entrance fee, so it's worth checking in advance.
- **Picnics and Dining**: While there are no large restaurants within the park, visitors can bring their own snacks and enjoy a picnic. However, there are cafés at the park's entrance and near the zoo that offer light refreshments.
- **Plan a Half-Day Visit**: To fully enjoy Belvedere Park, plan for at least 2–3 hours. You can leisurely explore the park, visit the zoo, and stop by the museum.
- **Transportation**: Belvedere Park is easily accessible from central Tunis. Taxis and public buses regularly service the area, making it a convenient spot to visit during your time in the city.

Cathedral of St. Vincent de Paul

The Cathedral of St. Vincent de Paul (Cathédrale Saint-Vincent-de-Paul de Tunis) is an iconic example of colonial-era architecture in Tunis. Located in the heart of the city, it stands as a symbol of Tunisia's diverse religious history, particularly its Christian heritage. Built in the early 20th century, the cathedral combines

Romanesque and Byzantine architectural styles, making it one of the most visually striking buildings in Tunis.

Key Features and Highlights:

1. **Architectural Design**:
   - The cathedral was designed by French architect **Louis Lequier** and completed in 1897. Its architectural style is a blend of Romanesque and Byzantine influences, with elements such as rounded arches, ornate columns, and an impressive rose window.
   - The cathedral features a distinctive **three-aisled nave**, a high vaulted ceiling, and numerous stained-glass windows that depict religious scenes. The façade is adorned with intricate carvings, and the central door is framed with ornate arches.
2. **Interior Decoration**:
   - Inside, the cathedral is equally impressive, with **beautiful mosaic floors** and **painted frescoes** that highlight scenes from the life of Saint Vincent de Paul. The high altar, surrounded by columns, is a focal point of the interior and is decorated with elaborate gold leaf details.
   - **Stained-glass windows** add a colorful touch to the interior, casting beautiful light patterns on the stone floor as the sun shines through. The windows depict saints, biblical scenes, and the Virgin Mary, with some windows featuring Arabic inscriptions alongside traditional Christian motifs.
3. **Cultural and Religious Significance**:

- The Cathedral of St. Vincent de Paul has long been a place of Christian worship, serving as a spiritual center for the small but significant Christian community in Tunis. Though the country is predominantly Muslim, the cathedral remains an important symbol of the multicultural heritage of Tunis.
- The church is named after **St. Vincent de Paul**, a 17th-century French priest known for his charitable works and dedication to helping the poor. His legacy is honored through the church's ongoing mission of providing support to local communities.

4. **Surrounding Area**:
   - The cathedral is situated on **Avenue Habib Bourguiba**, one of Tunis's most famous and busiest streets. This area is known for its colonial-era buildings, cafes, and shops, making the cathedral a perfect stop while exploring the heart of the city.
   - It is located near other important landmarks like the **National Theatre of Tunis** and **Tunis's City Hall**, offering visitors a chance to experience the city's cultural and architectural diversity.

Visitor Tips:

- **Opening Hours**: The cathedral is open to visitors throughout the week, but it's best to check for any special services or mass schedules, as these may limit visitor access.
- **Dress Code**: As the cathedral is an active place of worship, it's important to dress modestly. Women may be asked to

cover their shoulders and wear skirts or trousers below the knee.
- **Photography**: Photography is allowed inside the cathedral, but it's important to be respectful and avoid taking photos during religious ceremonies.
- **Peaceful Atmosphere**: Although the cathedral is located on a busy street, it offers a calm and peaceful environment inside. Take some time to sit and enjoy the tranquil ambiance, especially during the quieter hours of the day.

Habib Bourguiba Avenue

Habib Bourguiba Avenue (Avenue Habib Bourguiba) is the main thoroughfare of Tunis and one of the city's most iconic streets. Often referred to as the **"Champs-Élysées of Tunis,"** it is the epicenter of the city's cultural, political, and social life. Stretching from the **French colonial district** to the **Medina**, this wide boulevard is lined with grand colonial-era buildings, luxury hotels, cafés, and shops, making it a popular destination for both locals and tourists.

Key Features and Highlights:

1. **Colonial Architecture and Landmarks**:
   - The avenue is a showcase of **colonial-era architecture**, with many buildings reflecting French architectural influence. From **neoclassical** facades to **Art Deco** structures, the avenue offers a glimpse into the country's colonial past.
   - Important landmarks along the avenue include the **National Theatre of Tunis**, the **French Institute**, and the **City Hall**. These buildings, with their

distinctive architecture, make the avenue a hub of activity and a historical corridor that tells the story of Tunisia's transition from French protectorate to independent nation.

2. **The Bourguiba Monument**:
   - One of the most significant landmarks on the avenue is the **Bourguiba Monument**, which honors **Habib Bourguiba**, the first president of Tunisia and a key figure in the country's independence. The monument consists of a large bronze statue of Bourguiba in an iconic stance, symbolizing his leadership in the struggle for freedom and modernization.
   - The statue is located in the central square of the avenue, offering a powerful symbol of Tunisia's national identity and its journey toward independence.

3. **Cafés and Shopping**:
   - The avenue is known for its **cafés**, which are popular spots for both locals and tourists to relax and people-watch. Many of these cafés have **outdoor terraces** where visitors can enjoy a cup of traditional Tunisian coffee or mint tea while soaking in the lively atmosphere of the avenue.
   - For shoppers, **Habib Bourguiba Avenue** is a vibrant hub, offering a range of **international boutiques**, **local shops**, and **bookstores**. This is a great place to purchase souvenirs, including

Tunisian handicrafts, perfumes, and traditional clothing.

4. **Cultural and Historical Significance**:
   - Habib Bourguiba Avenue is named after **Habib Bourguiba**, who played a pivotal role in the country's fight for independence and in shaping modern Tunisia. As the first president of Tunisia, Bourguiba's vision of progress and his push for secularism are reflected in the monuments and public spaces along the avenue.
   - The avenue is a focal point for national celebrations and protests, making it a site of political significance in modern Tunis. It has hosted numerous demonstrations, including the 2011 protests that led to the fall of President Ben Ali's regime.

Visitor Tips:

- **Best Time to Visit**: Habib Bourguiba Avenue is a busy street throughout the day, but it comes alive in the late afternoon and evening when locals gather at the cafés and the atmosphere becomes vibrant and festive.
- **Walking and Exploring**: The avenue is best explored on foot. Take time to admire the architecture, visit the nearby historical landmarks, and enjoy the various cafes and shops. Walking also allows you to soak in the bustling energy of the area.
- **Dining Options**: The avenue offers plenty of **restaurants and cafés** that serve both Tunisian and international cuisine. Whether you're in the mood for traditional dishes

like **couscous** or more contemporary offerings, there's a dining option for every taste.
- **Public Transport**: Habib Bourguiba Avenue is well-connected by public transport, including buses and the Tunis Metro. Taxis are also readily available, making it easy to explore the area.

Dar Ben Abdallah Museum

The **Dar Ben Abdallah Museum** is an important historical and cultural landmark in the heart of Tunis, located within the old **Medina** (historic center of the city). This museum offers visitors a glimpse into the traditional Tunisian way of life, showcasing the art, culture, and domestic architecture of the 18th and 19th centuries.

Key Features and Highlights:

1. **Historical Significance**:
   - The Dar Ben Abdallah building itself is an excellent example of traditional Tunisian architecture. It was once the residence of a wealthy family during the 18th century and later became a museum to preserve the cultural heritage of Tunis.
   - The house is named after **Ben Abdallah**, a former owner, and is typical of the wealthy homes of the era, featuring a rich mix of **Arabic, Andalusian, and Ottoman** influences.
2. **Architectural Design**:
   - The museum is housed in a stunning **traditional Dar** (house), which is built around a central courtyard with a beautifully tiled **fountain**. The

walls of the rooms are adorned with colorful **zellij** (traditional Tunisian tiles), and wooden windows have intricate carvings, a typical feature of Tunisian architecture.
- The **mosaic floors**, painted wooden ceilings, and decorative **stucco work** in the building reflect the sophistication and opulence of the period. The private rooms, courtyards, and passageways offer a detailed look at the lifestyle of the elite in 18th-century Tunisia.

3. **Exhibits and Collections**:
   - Inside the museum, visitors can explore a collection of **traditional Tunisian crafts**, including **textiles**, **pottery**, **furniture**, and **glassware**. The museum showcases local handicrafts, which were often used in daily life, as well as decorative arts that reflect the cultural influences of various periods.
   - The museum also highlights **costumes** worn by the wealthy during the period, displaying elaborate **Tunisia dresses**, traditional jewelry, and accessories that were common in Tunisian society.
   - There is also a display of **old household items** such as **ceramics**, **brassware**, and **silver**, which help illustrate the domestic lives of affluent families at the time.

4. **Cultural Education**:
   - The museum is an important educational space, where visitors can learn about **Tunisian history**, **architecture**, and **domestic life** from the 18th and 19th centuries. The museum often hosts cultural events, temporary exhibitions, and workshops that

focus on preserving and celebrating Tunisia's rich heritage.
- It is an excellent place for those interested in learning more about the **traditional arts and crafts** of Tunisia, as it serves to preserve the country's cultural traditions while educating the public about its past.

5. **Museum Layout**:
    - The museum is divided into several rooms, each offering a different aspect of traditional Tunisian life. Visitors can explore the **courtyards**, **reception rooms**, and **private family chambers**, each decorated with period furnishings and artifacts that were once used by the elite class.
    - The **main salon** and **dining area** offer a glimpse into the grandeur of social gatherings, featuring elaborate seating arrangements and tables set with antique silverware.

Visitor Tips:

- **Opening Hours**: The museum is generally open daily, except for certain public holidays, but it's always a good idea to check ahead for specific opening times. It is usually quieter in the mornings, making it a great time to visit if you prefer to avoid crowds.
- **Guided Tours**: Consider taking a **guided tour** of the museum for a more enriching experience. Knowledgeable guides can provide deeper insights into the history, cultural context, and significance of the exhibits.
- **Dress Modestly**: As with other museums in Tunisia, it's recommended to dress modestly, especially since it's

situated in the Medina, which is a historically conservative area.
- **Nearby Attractions**: The museum is located within walking distance of other key landmarks in the Medina, including **Zitouna Mosque** and the **Souks** (markets). It's a great addition to a full-day exploration of the Medina area.

La Goulette

La Goulette (or **Goulette**) is a charming coastal town located just a few kilometers from Tunis, on the Mediterranean Sea. Historically, La Goulette was an important port town and the gateway to Tunis, welcoming travelers and merchants from across the Mediterranean. Today, it is a lively, picturesque area that combines its historic maritime past with modern-day attractions.

Key Features and Highlights:

1. **Historic Port and Waterfront**:
   - La Goulette has a long history as a trading port, and its harbor remains a key feature of the town. The port is still active today, with numerous fishing boats and ferries operating in and out of the area.
   - The waterfront is lined with palm trees and offers lovely views of the Mediterranean Sea. Visitors can stroll along the **beachfront promenade**, enjoy the breeze, and watch the bustling harbor activity.
2. **Rich Cultural Heritage**:
   - La Goulette was historically a **multicultural hub**, with a mix of Muslim, Christian, and Jewish populations. This diversity is reflected in the town's architecture, cuisine, and daily life.

- One of the most notable cultural elements of La Goulette is its **Ottoman heritage**, visible in the **mosques**, **villages**, and **colonial-era buildings** that line the streets. The town was a popular retreat for wealthy Tunisians and foreigners, and this heritage adds to the charm of the area.

3. **The Medina of La Goulette**:
    - The town's old district, the **Medina of La Goulette**, is home to narrow streets, vibrant markets, and traditional shops. Visitors can explore local **souks** selling fresh seafood, spices, handmade goods, and Tunisian textiles.
    - The area is also home to some beautiful **Ottoman-style buildings**, including several well-preserved **mosques** and **palaces**.

4. **Beaches and Resorts**:
    - La Goulette is also famous for its **beaches**. The coastline here is ideal for relaxing by the sea, with soft sand and clear waters. It's a popular destination for both local and international tourists who want to enjoy the Mediterranean climate.
    - Several **beach resorts** and **restaurants** are situated along the shore, offering a mix of seafood and local dishes. The beach is perfect for sunbathing, swimming, or enjoying a quiet afternoon by the sea.

5. **Dining and Nightlife**:
    - La Goulette is known for its **seafood cuisine**, with numerous restaurants serving **fresh fish, shellfish**, and **grilled seafood dishes**. Visitors should not miss the opportunity to try **Tunisian-style seafood couscous** or a traditional **fish tagine**.

- The area also has a lively **nightlife**, with cafes, bars, and lounges along the coast, making it a great place for an evening out, especially during the summer months.

6. **Religious and Historical Sites**:
    - La Goulette is home to several **religious sites**, including **churches** and **synagogues**, reflecting its diverse past. The **church of St. Louis** is a notable landmark in the area, built by the French during the colonial period.
    - The town is also close to the **Carthage ruins**, one of Tunisia's most significant historical sites, which can easily be visited from La Goulette.

Visitor Tips:

- **Getting There**: La Goulette is easily accessible by public transport from Tunis, with both buses and taxis regularly operating between the capital and the port town. Alternatively, the area can be reached by **train** from central Tunis to the La Goulette station.
- **Best Time to Visit**: The best time to visit La Goulette is during the spring and fall when the weather is mild. The summer months can get quite hot, and the beaches are often crowded.
- **Family-Friendly**: La Goulette is an ideal destination for families, with its combination of beaches, parks, and local attractions. Children can enjoy swimming in the sea or exploring the Medina and harbor area.
- **Local Cuisine**: Don't miss out on the town's famous seafood dishes. Visit one of the many seaside restaurants for a meal with a view of the Mediterranean Sea.

Conclusion on Top Attractions in Tunis

Tunis offers a wealth of experiences that highlight its historical, cultural, and architectural significance. The city's top attractions not only showcase Tunisia's rich past but also its dynamic present, making it an ideal destination for those seeking to explore a blend of tradition and modernity. Whether you're wandering through the narrow streets of the Medina, admiring the majestic landmarks, or enjoying the Mediterranean coastline, Tunis remains a city that leaves a lasting impression on every visitor.

Top Beaches in Tunis

Tunis, Tunisia's vibrant capital, offers a blend of rich history, cultural landmarks, and stunning beaches. With the Mediterranean coastline just a short distance from the city, tourists can easily access a variety of beaches that range from lively and bustling to quiet and secluded. This guide explores the top beaches in and around Tunis, providing essential information and tips for a memorable beach experience.

La Marsa Beach

- **Location**: Just 15 kilometers north of central Tunis, La Marsa is one of the most popular beaches for locals and tourists alike.
- **Overview**: Known for its golden sands and clear waters, La Marsa Beach is a blend of relaxation and local culture. Its prime location makes it easily accessible and ideal for a quick beach escape from the city. The beach is family-friendly and offers plenty of amenities, including cafés,

shops, and easy access to nearby attractions like Sidi Bou Said.
- **Highlights**:
  - **Ideal for swimming and sunbathing**: Calm waters make it suitable for all ages.
  - **Seaside cafés**: Numerous establishments along the beach serve refreshing drinks, seafood, and Tunisian snacks.
  - **Proximity to cultural sites**: La Marsa is close to historical gems like Sidi Bou Said, a picturesque town known for its blue-and-white architecture.
  - **Vibrant atmosphere**: The beach comes alive in the evenings, with people strolling along the promenade or gathering at local spots.
- **Tips**:
  - Visit early in the morning or late afternoon to avoid the crowds.
  - La Marsa's public beach areas are free, but for more comfort, consider renting a spot at a private beach club for access to amenities like loungers and umbrellas.
  - If you're planning to spend an entire day at the beach, bring sun protection and water, as the midday sun can be intense.

Gammarth Beach

- **Location**: Around 20 kilometers north of Tunis, in the upscale area of Gammarth.
- **Overview**: Gammarth Beach offers a more luxurious beach experience with its upscale resorts and exclusive atmosphere. This beach is well-known for its clear, blue

waters and is perfect for travelers seeking comfort and tranquility away from the more crowded areas.
- **Highlights**:
  - **Private beach clubs**: Access to well-maintained, exclusive sections of the beach through resorts that provide amenities such as loungers, umbrellas, and beachside service.
  - **Water sports**: Enjoy activities like jet skiing, parasailing, and windsurfing in the calm, clear waters.
  - **Luxury resorts**: Stay in one of the many high-end hotels that offer beachfront views and direct access to the water.
  - **Great for relaxation**: With its peaceful surroundings and well-kept environment, Gammarth is ideal for unwinding and enjoying a more luxurious beach experience.
- **Tips**:
  - If you're not staying at a resort, you can still access the beach by paying for entry to a private beach club.
  - Visit in the early morning or evening to enjoy the serene beauty before the crowds arrive.
  - Gammarth has a sophisticated vibe, so dress in comfortable yet stylish clothing if planning to dine or visit the resorts.

Raoued Beach

- **Location**: Located about 25 kilometers northeast of Tunis, Raoued Beach is a more tranquil alternative to the popular urban beaches.

- **Overview**: Known for its natural beauty and unspoiled environment, Raoued Beach is a peaceful retreat. The clear waters and clean sand make it a perfect destination for those looking to escape the crowds and enjoy a quieter beach experience.
- **Highlights**:
    - **Seclusion and natural beauty**: Raoued Beach offers a more relaxed, secluded atmosphere with fewer tourists.
    - **Local fishing villages**: The beach is surrounded by traditional fishing communities, offering a glimpse into Tunisian coastal life.
    - **Great for sunbathing and swimming**: The beach is perfect for those who prefer peace and quiet while enjoying the Mediterranean sun.
    - **Picnics and relaxation**: The serene environment is ideal for those who wish to enjoy a relaxed day by the sea, perhaps with a picnic on the sand.
- **Tips**:
    - Bring your own food and drinks as there are limited facilities around the beach.
    - The beach can be windy, so it's ideal for kite surfing or windsurfing if you're into water sports.
    - It's a good idea to visit Raoued on weekdays when the beach is quieter, particularly during the summer months.

Hammamet Beach

- **Location**: Approximately 60 kilometers southeast of Tunis, in the popular resort town of Hammamet.

- **Overview**: Hammamet Beach is one of Tunisia's most iconic beaches, known for its beautiful setting and lively atmosphere. With a mix of clear waters, fine sand, and bustling promenades, it's perfect for those seeking both relaxation and entertainment. Hammamet has long been a favorite destination for international tourists.
- **Highlights**:
  - **Wide sandy stretch**: Hammamet Beach offers a long, spacious coastline, great for swimming, sunbathing, and beach sports.
  - **Vibrant promenade**: The beach is surrounded by shops, restaurants, and beach clubs where you can dine or enjoy a drink by the sea.
  - **Water sports**: Popular activities include parasailing, water skiing, and jet skiing.
  - **Nightlife**: The town comes alive in the evening, with beach bars and live music events providing entertainment after the sun sets.
- **Tips**:
  - Hammamet Beach can be crowded, especially in high season. To avoid the crowds, consider visiting early or during the off-peak months (April-May or September-October).
  - Be cautious of the local vendors, as they may approach you on the beach. If you're not interested in buying anything, politely decline.
  - If you're traveling with children, Hammamet is a great choice due to its shallow waters and family-friendly atmosphere.

Nabeul Beach

- **Location**: Around 60 kilometers southeast of Tunis, in the coastal town of Nabeul.
- **Overview**: Nabeul Beach combines a rich cultural experience with a relaxing beach setting. Known for its pottery and handicrafts, Nabeul is a wonderful destination for travelers who want to enjoy the beach while also exploring local markets and artisan workshops.
- **Highlights**:
    - **Shallow, calm waters**: Ideal for families and those who enjoy swimming in gentle seas.
    - **Cultural experience**: Nabeul is famous for its pottery, so you can explore local shops and buy handcrafted ceramics as souvenirs.
    - **Pleasant promenade**: Nabeul Beach is lined with palm trees, offering a nice place to stroll or relax in the shade.
    - **Nearby market**: Nabeul's market is perfect for shopping for local products, including pottery, textiles, and spices.

- **Tips**:
    - Make time to visit the pottery workshops in Nabeul for a hands-on cultural experience.
    - Take a walk around the market, but be prepared to haggle for the best prices.
    - If you're planning to stay longer, check out the nearby hotels and resorts for a complete Tunisian coastal getaway.

Korbous Hot Springs Beach

- **Location**: About 60 kilometers northeast of Tunis, near the village of Korbous.
- **Overview**: Korbous is famous for its natural hot springs, which are believed to have therapeutic properties. The beach here offers the unique experience of soaking in warm spring waters while enjoying the Mediterranean Sea.
- **Highlights**:
    - **Thermal baths**: The hot springs are perfect for relaxing and rejuvenating after a swim.
    - **Secluded location**: Korbous is less crowded than other beaches around Tunis, making it ideal for a peaceful escape.
    - **Scenic surroundings**: The area is surrounded by hills and cliffs, offering stunning views and a tranquil environment.
    - **Nature lovers' paradise**: The beach is located in a more natural and less-developed part of the coast, providing a serene atmosphere.
- **Tips**:
    - Bring your own towels and swimwear for the thermal baths.
    - The beach has limited amenities, so it's a good idea to pack your own snacks and drinks.
    - If you enjoy hiking or nature walks, consider exploring the surrounding hills for panoramic views of the coastline.

Tips for Visiting Beaches in Tunis

- **Best Time to Visit**: The ideal time to visit Tunisian beaches is during the spring (April-May) and autumn (September-October), when the weather is warm but not

overly hot. Summer (June-August) can be very hot and crowded.
- **What to Pack**: Sunscreen, hats, sunglasses, beach towels, swimwear, and water shoes for some rocky coastal areas are essential. If you're visiting more secluded beaches, bring your own food and water.
- **Transportation**: Most beaches around Tunis are easily accessible by taxi or public transportation. Renting a car is recommended if you want to explore more remote beaches.

Tunis offers a wide variety of beaches that cater to all types of travelers—from those looking for lively beach scenes to those in search of tranquil, natural retreats. Whether you're in the mood for water sports, relaxing by the sea, or exploring cultural landmarks, the beaches around Tunis promise an unforgettable Mediterranean escape.

OUTDOOR ACTIVITIES AND ADVENTURES IN TUNIS

Tunis offers a diverse range of outdoor experiences, combining natural beauty, historical landmarks, and vibrant local culture. From exploring ancient ruins to enjoying leisurely seaside strolls, outdoor enthusiasts will find plenty to indulge in.

Hiking in Tunis

Tunis may not have towering mountains or dramatic landscapes like some other destinations, but it offers a range of fascinating hiking opportunities, allowing you to experience its rich history and natural beauty up close.

Popular Hiking Trails in Tunis and Surroundings

1. **Carthage Hills Hike**
    - **Location**: Carthage
    - **Overview**: The ancient hilltops of Carthage offer stunning views of the Mediterranean and the ruins of this historic city. The trail takes you through archaeological sites like Byrsa Hill, the Antonine Baths, and the Punic Ports, allowing hikers to combine natural beauty with historical exploration.
    - **Difficulty**: Moderate
    - **Distance**: Approximately 5-6 km
    - **Tips**: Bring water and sunscreen, as the route is exposed to the sun. Start your hike in the early morning or late afternoon to avoid the heat.

2. **Ichkeul National Park**
   - **Location**: North of Tunis, near Bizerte
   - **Overview**: Ichkeul National Park is a UNESCO World Heritage Site known for its biodiversity and scenic beauty. The park is home to a large lake, wetlands, and mountains. Hiking through this area allows you to explore a variety of habitats, including wetlands and forested hills. It's also an excellent spot for birdwatching, especially during the migration season.
   - **Difficulty**: Easy to moderate
   - **Distance**: Varies (easy to medium-length trails)
   - **Tips**: Bring binoculars for birdwatching, especially in autumn and spring when migratory birds pass through. Wear comfortable shoes for walking through varied terrain.
3. **Jebel Zaghouan**
   - **Location**: South of Tunis, near the town of Zaghouan
   - **Overview**: Jebel Zaghouan is a mountain offering a challenging hike with panoramic views of the surrounding countryside. The hike to the summit is well worth the effort, as you can see the remnants of the ancient Roman water system, which once supplied water to Carthage. At the top, enjoy sweeping views of the Mediterranean and the surrounding hills.
   - **Difficulty**: Moderate to difficult
   - **Distance**: 7-8 km round trip
   - **Tips**: Make sure to bring plenty of water and wear appropriate hiking boots. The trail can be steep in parts, so it's recommended for more experienced hikers.
4. **La Marsa Coastal Trail**
   - **Location**: Coastal area near Tunis

- **Overview**: For a more relaxed, scenic hike, head to the coastal path near La Marsa. This easy trail offers beautiful views of the Mediterranean and is perfect for a sunset hike. The walk stretches along the coast, passing through charming coastal villages and secluded beaches.
- **Difficulty**: Easy
- **Distance**: 3-4 km
- **Tips**: Ideal for a morning or evening walk. It's perfect for casual hikers, families, or those looking for a less strenuous experience.

Essential Hiking Tips for Tunis

- **Weather Considerations**: Tunisian summers can be very hot, especially in the midday sun, so it's essential to start your hikes early in the morning or later in the afternoon to avoid the heat. Winters can be mild, but rain is possible, so always check the weather forecast before heading out.
- **Hydration**: Always carry water with you, especially on longer hikes, as water sources are limited in some areas.
- **Footwear**: Depending on the terrain, sturdy, comfortable shoes or hiking boots are necessary. Some trails may be rocky or uneven, so choose your footwear accordingly.
- **Guided Hikes**: If you're unfamiliar with the trails, it's a good idea to hire a local guide. They can provide insights into the natural and cultural significance of the areas you're exploring and ensure you stay on track.

Sailing in Tunis

The Mediterranean Sea surrounding Tunis provides ideal conditions for sailing, with clear waters, gentle breezes, and stunning coastal views. Sailing here combines a rich historical context, as you glide past ancient ruins and vibrant harbors, with an opportunity to relax and enjoy the peaceful waters.

Popular Sailing Routes and Experiences

1. **Tunis Bay and La Marsa**
   - **Overview**: This is one of the most popular sailing routes for tourists. Starting from the vibrant port of La Marsa, sail along the coastline and enjoy spectacular views of the city and the sea. You'll pass beautiful beaches and rocky coves before heading out to Tunis Bay, where you can anchor and enjoy a swim in the crystal-clear waters.
   - **Duration**: 2-4 hours
   - **Highlights**: Views of Tunisian architecture, the shoreline, and iconic landmarks like the ruins of Carthage.
   - **Tips**: A great route for beginner sailors or those looking for a relaxing day on the water.
2. **Sidi Bou Said to Cap Bon Peninsula**
   - **Overview**: A more adventurous sailing option, this route takes you from the picturesque village of Sidi Bou Said along the stunning Cap Bon Peninsula. The journey offers breathtaking views of the Mediterranean coastline, where you can stop to explore hidden beaches and coves.
   - **Duration**: Half-day to full-day excursions

- **Highlights**: Beautiful natural landscapes, secluded beaches, and the chance to spot marine life.
- **Tips**: Be sure to bring a camera for the scenic views, and consider a guide to ensure you don't miss the best spots.

3. **Carthage and the Gulf of Tunis**
   - **Overview**: For a historical sailing experience, consider a trip from the harbor of Carthage, exploring the Gulf of Tunis. This excursion offers views of both ancient ruins and vibrant modern-day Tunis, creating a unique contrast between history and contemporary life.
   - **Duration**: 3-5 hours
   - **Highlights**: The ancient harbor of Carthage, panoramic views of Tunis, and the historical backdrop of the city.
   - **Tips**: Sail in the morning or late afternoon to avoid strong midday sun and enjoy cooler breezes.

Sailing Tips for Beginners and Experienced Sailors

- **Safety**: Always ensure that the boat is equipped with the necessary safety equipment, including life jackets, fire extinguishers, and first aid kits. Confirm that the captain is certified and experienced.
- **What to Bring**: Sunscreen, a hat, sunglasses, a camera, and a bottle of water are essential for staying comfortable during your time on the water.
- **Seasickness**: If you're prone to seasickness, it's a good idea to take preventative measures (like seasickness tablets) before setting sail.

Fishing Excursions in Tunis

For fishing enthusiasts, Tunis offers a range of fishing experiences, from tranquil inshore trips to thrilling deep-sea fishing expeditions. The waters off the coast are teeming with a variety of fish species, including tuna, dorado, and groupers, making it an ideal destination for both casual anglers and serious fishermen.

Popular Fishing Excursions in Tunis

1. **Deep-Sea Fishing from La Goulette**
   - **Overview**: La Goulette, a busy port just outside of Tunis, is a popular starting point for deep-sea fishing excursions. Here, you'll have the opportunity to head out into the deeper Mediterranean waters where you can fish for larger species like tuna, dorado, and barracuda.
   - **Duration**: Half-day (4-5 hours) or full-day (7-8 hours) trips
   - **Highlights**: Catching larger fish species, experiencing the thrill of deep-sea fishing, and exploring the open Mediterranean.
   - **Tips**: Make sure to book in advance, especially during the peak fishing season (spring and summer). If you're a beginner, opt for a guided tour to learn the basics of deep-sea fishing.
2. **Coastal Fishing from Sidi Bou Said**
   - **Overview**: If you're looking for a more relaxed fishing experience, consider a coastal fishing trip from the charming village of Sidi Bou Said. These excursions are typically shorter and focus on catching smaller species like snapper and bream.

This type of fishing is perfect for families or anyone new to the sport.
- **Duration**: 2-3 hours
- **Highlights**: Calm waters, great for beginners and families, and the chance to fish right off the coast while enjoying beautiful views.
- **Tips**: Coastal fishing is generally less taxing and great for catching fish for a casual meal. Be sure to bring some snacks and drinks for a leisurely afternoon.

3. **Tuna Fishing in the Mediterranean**
   - **Overview**: Tunisia is well-known for its bluefin tuna, which can be found in abundance in the Mediterranean. Bluefin tuna fishing is a challenging and exciting experience for those seeking an adrenaline rush.
   - **Duration**: Full-day trip (8-10 hours)
   - **Highlights**: Bluefin tuna, one of the largest and most sought-after fish species in the world, known for its size and strength.
   - **Tips**: Tuna fishing is often best in the late summer and fall, and due to the nature of the fish, this type of excursion is best suited for experienced anglers or those who are looking for a real challenge.

Fishing Tips for Success

- **Licenses and Regulations**: Always check with your operator to ensure you have the correct permits for fishing, as there may be restrictions on certain species or areas.
- **Equipment**: Most tour operators provide all necessary fishing equipment, including rods, reels, and bait. However,

if you have your own gear, bring it along for a more personalized experience.
- **Best Time to Fish**: The best time to fish in Tunis is from April to October, with peak fishing seasons during the warmer months when the Mediterranean waters are teeming with fish.
- **Local Guides**: If you're not familiar with the area, hiring a local fishing guide can enhance your experience. They know the best fishing spots and can provide expert advice on techniques and bait.

Cycling Adventures in Tunis

Tunis offers a fantastic landscape for cycling enthusiasts, whether you're an experienced cyclist looking for a challenging route or a casual traveler interested in exploring the city and surrounding nature at a slower pace. From the bustling streets of the city to the tranquil coastal paths and rural roads leading to stunning natural landscapes, Tunis provides diverse cycling opportunities that will appeal to a wide range of riders. Here's a comprehensive guide to cycling adventures in and around Tunis.

Cycling in the City of Tunis

Cycling around the city of Tunis gives you a unique opportunity to explore the bustling streets, historic neighborhoods, and vibrant markets in an eco-friendly and active way. While Tunis may not have extensive bike lanes like some other major cities, it is still a great place to experience the heart of Tunisia's capital.

Suggested Cycling Routes in Tunis

1. **Medina of Tunis**

- Overview: The Medina is a UNESCO World Heritage Site, with narrow, winding streets, ancient mosques, souks (markets), and historical buildings. Cycling through the Medina is an incredible way to experience Tunis' historical charm, allowing you to reach sites like the Zitouna Mosque and Bab el Bhar (Porte de France) in a more leisurely way.
        - Route Description: Start from the Place de la République and cycle into the Medina, exploring its alleys and landmarks. The streets are quite busy, so it's advisable to cycle cautiously.
        - Best Time: Early mornings or late afternoons are ideal to avoid crowds and the midday heat.
2. **Carthage to Sidi Bou Said**
        - Overview: This scenic coastal route takes you from the ancient ruins of Carthage to the charming, white-and-blue village of Sidi Bou Said. It's a relatively short but delightful ride with a mix of urban streets and coastal paths, offering beautiful views of the Mediterranean.
        - Route Description: Begin in Carthage and cycle towards the hillside village of Sidi Bou Said. The route takes you past archaeological sites and along the coastal roads, where you'll be able to enjoy panoramic sea views and the iconic Mediterranean architecture of Sidi Bou Said.
        - Distance: Approximately 7 kilometers (4.3 miles)
        - Best Time: Early morning or sunset when the temperatures are cooler and the views are more dramatic.

3. **Lac de Tunis (Lake Tunis)**

- **Overview**: If you're looking for a peaceful ride outside the city, a route around Lake Tunis is a great choice. The area surrounding the lake offers scenic views, calm waters, and a quieter cycling environment.
- **Route Description**: You can start from the northern side of the lake and cycle along its perimeter, passing through rural roads and small villages. This is a relaxing ride that's suitable for cyclists of all levels, and you may also spot some birdlife around the lake.
- **Distance**: Approximately 15 kilometers (9.3 miles)
- **Best Time**: The cooler months of spring and autumn are perfect for this ride.

Cycling Tours and Guided Expeditions

For travelers who prefer to explore Tunis with the help of a local guide or seek a more structured cycling adventure, there are several cycling tours and guided expeditions available that can take you to some of the city's highlights, as well as into the surrounding countryside and coastal areas.

Popular Cycling Tours in Tunis

1. **Cultural Bike Tour of Tunis**
   - **Overview**: This guided tour takes you on a journey through Tunis' rich cultural history, cycling from the modern parts of the city to the ancient Medina. A knowledgeable guide will introduce you to the history of the city, its culture, and the significance of the landmarks you visit.
   - **Duration**: 3-4 hours

- **Highlights**: Key attractions such as the Medina, the Bardo Museum (if included), and the picturesque souks.
- **Best Time**: Morning tours are typically cooler and less crowded.

2. **Sidi Bou Said and Carthage Archaeological Ride**
   - **Overview**: This tour focuses on the archaeological wonders of Carthage and the quaint village of Sidi Bou Said. The route provides a great mix of cultural exploration and cycling, perfect for history lovers.
   - **Duration**: 4-5 hours
   - **Highlights**: The ancient ruins of Carthage, the blue-and-white village of Sidi Bou Said, and sweeping views of the Mediterranean.
   - **Best Time**: Early morning or late afternoon.

3. **Coastal Cycling Tour to La Marsa**
   - **Overview**: If you want to experience more of the Mediterranean coastline, a cycling tour to La Marsa is a great option. The route offers scenic views, cool sea breezes, and beautiful beaches.
   - **Duration**: 3-4 hours
   - **Highlights**: The coastal road from Tunis to La Marsa, with stops at beaches and local cafés for a taste of Tunisian life.
   - **Best Time**: Morning rides are ideal for cooler temperatures and fewer crowds.

Cycling Beyond Tunis

For those who are looking for a more adventurous cycling experience, the areas surrounding Tunis provide scenic routes through forests, mountains, and agricultural lands. These routes are ideal for cyclists who want to experience the natural beauty of Tunisia away from the urban environment.

Cycling in the Tunisian Countryside

1. **Zaghouan and the Atlas Mountains**
   - **Overview**: If you're up for a more challenging ride, cycling in the Zaghouan area, located about 50 kilometers from Tunis, offers beautiful mountain scenery and rural landscapes. The Atlas Mountains offer a mix of tough terrain, rocky roads, and panoramic views.
   - **Route Description**: Begin in the town of Zaghouan and cycle into the surrounding foothills and mountain trails. The area is known for its Roman ruins, including the remains of the ancient Roman aqueduct.
   - **Difficulty**: Intermediate to advanced due to the hilly terrain.
   - **Best Time**: Spring and autumn are the best times to visit, with pleasant weather for cycling in the mountains.
2. **Ksar Ouled Soltane (Southern Tunisia)**
   - **Overview**: For those seeking an off-the-beaten-path adventure, cycling in the south of Tunisia offers a desert-like environment with stunning landscapes. Ksar Ouled Soltane, located in the region of Tataouine, is a famous location for cycling tours.
   - **Route Description**: Start from Tataouine and cycle through the arid landscapes, passing through ancient ksars (fortified villages) and palm groves.
   - **Difficulty**: Advanced cyclists will enjoy this challenge, as it involves rough terrain and long rides in the desert.

- o **Best Time**: Early spring or late autumn to avoid the extreme heat.

Cycling Tips and Essentials

- **What to Bring**:
  - o A helmet is essential for safety, as cycling in urban areas can be challenging.
  - o Comfortable cycling clothing, including padded shorts for long rides.
  - o Water bottles to stay hydrated, especially during the summer months.
  - o A map or GPS, especially if you're venturing out on your own to rural areas or along unfamiliar routes.
- **Bike Rentals**: Bikes can be rented from local shops in Tunis and at bike tour companies. Ensure you rent a high-quality bike suited to your needs (mountain, road, or hybrid).
- **Safety Tips**: In the city, always be cautious of traffic, as some roads may not have dedicated bike lanes. Wearing bright clothing and using a bike light is recommended for visibility, especially if cycling at dusk or early morning.

Why Choose Cycling in Tunis?

Cycling in Tunis and the surrounding areas offers an excellent way to see the city and its surroundings at a leisurely pace. Whether you're exploring the historical sights within the Medina, taking in coastal views, or heading out into the rural countryside, cycling allows you to experience Tunisia from a unique perspective. It's an eco-friendly and active way to travel that allows for greater flexibility and more intimate exploration of this fascinating country. With diverse routes and experiences, cycling in Tunis caters to both beginners and experienced cyclists alike, making it an adventure that everyone can enjoy.

Desert Excursions Near Tunis

Tunis, with its proximity to Tunisia's expansive Sahara Desert, offers a gateway to some of the most breathtaking desert landscapes in North Africa. While the true Sahara begins further south, the desert regions near Tunis provide a unique blend of arid beauty, historic sites, and a chance to experience the timeless allure of the desert. From camel treks to off-road adventures, there are numerous opportunities to explore the surrounding desert regions.

Key Desert Destinations Near Tunis

1. **Chott el Jerid**
    - **Overview**: Chott el Jerid is one of the largest salt flats in the world, located about 350 kilometers south of Tunis. This vast expanse of cracked earth and salt is a surreal landscape, often described as a "moon-like" desert. It offers a unique, otherworldly atmosphere perfect for photography and adventure.
    - **What to Expect**: A visit to Chott el Jerid allows you to explore the salt plains on foot or by 4x4. You'll also pass through small desert villages, including Nefta, which is known for its picturesque palm groves. The area is also famous for being a filming location for *Star Wars*, with parts of the Tatooine scenes being shot here.
    - **Activities**:
        - **4x4 Desert Safari**: Take a thrilling 4x4 ride across the salt flats, which can include stops at

remote oases and the opportunity to see unique wildlife.
- **Camel Trekking**: For a more traditional experience, camel trekking through the salt flats and surrounding dunes is available, offering a chance to embrace the stillness of the desert.
- **Sunset Photography**: The best time to visit Chott el Jerid is at sunset when the landscape's colors change dramatically, offering excellent photo opportunities.

2. **Douz – Gateway to the Sahara**
   - **Overview**: Known as the "Gateway to the Sahara," Douz is a small town about 500 kilometers south of Tunis. It's located on the edge of the great desert and is the starting point for many desert excursions into the dunes of the Sahara. Douz is famous for its annual festival, the "Festival of the Sahara," where nomads gather to showcase traditional culture, music, and camel races.
   - **What to Expect**: Douz is a vibrant desert town with a strong cultural heritage. Visitors can explore the bustling souks (markets), where you can buy traditional Berber crafts, jewelry, and spices. From Douz, you can embark on desert adventures that take you deeper into the Sahara.
   - **Activities**:
     - **Camel Treks**: Douz offers camel treks that range from short rides to multi-day journeys into the desert, where you can spend the night under the stars.

- **Jeep Tours**: 4x4 jeep tours are popular for exploring the surrounding dunes, where you can experience the thrill of off-roading and visit remote oases like the ones near Ksar Ghilane.
- **Festival of the Sahara**: If you visit during the winter months (usually in December), the Festival of the Sahara in Douz is a unique cultural experience, showcasing desert traditions, music, and dance.

3. **Ksar Ghilane**
   - **Overview**: Ksar Ghilane is an oasis located approximately 320 kilometers south of Tunis, known for its stunning palm groves, hot springs, and its location at the edge of the Great Eastern Erg, the largest area of sand dunes in the Sahara. Ksar Ghilane is one of the most popular desert destinations, offering an authentic taste of desert life.
   - **What to Expect**: This peaceful oasis is perfect for those seeking a tranquil desert experience. Visitors can enjoy the warm waters of the hot springs or take part in activities that immerse them in desert culture and natural beauty.
   - **Activities**:
     - **Camel Rides**: Enjoy a relaxing camel ride through the surrounding sand dunes or visit the nearby ancient ruins of Tamerza, a village that was once part of the Berber caravan route.
     - **Hot Springs**: Take a dip in the natural hot springs, believed to have therapeutic properties.

It's a perfect way to relax after a long day of exploring the desert.
- **4x4 Off-Road Tours**: For the adventurous, 4x4 tours through the desert dunes provide an adrenaline-packed way to experience the Sahara's dramatic landscapes.

4. **Tamerza and the Mides Gorge**
    - **Overview**: Tamerza, located in the southern part of Tunisia, is an ancient mountain oasis town famous for its stunning landscapes and dramatic canyons. The nearby Mides Gorge, with its rocky cliffs and narrow passageways, adds a sense of adventure to the desert journey.
    - **What to Expect**: Tamerza is known for its terraced olive groves and traditional adobe houses that stand against the backdrop of the surrounding desert. The Mides Gorge is a great spot for hiking, offering rugged terrain and stunning views of the surrounding area.
    - **Activities**:
        - **Hiking and Trekking**: Explore the Mides Gorge and Tamerza on foot, taking in the dramatic landscape and the contrast between the lush oasis and the surrounding arid desert.
        - **Photography**: The landscapes of Tamerza and Mides Gorge are perfect for photography, especially the combination of desert cliffs, palm trees, and the unique architecture of the village.
        - **Cultural Visits**: Tamerza offers a glimpse into the desert's traditional life, with Berber villages, old ksars (fortified buildings), and the chance to

meet locals who still follow age-old desert customs.

Types of Desert Activities Near Tunis

1. **Camel Treks**
   - Camel treks are one of the most iconic desert experiences in Tunisia. Most desert excursions from Tunis offer camel rides, which can vary in duration from short rides around oases to multi-day treks into the heart of the Sahara. These treks offer an authentic way to explore the desert, allowing you to experience the peacefulness of the landscape, sleep under the stars, and learn about traditional desert life.

2. **4x4 Off-Road Adventures**
   - For a more adrenaline-filled experience, 4x4 off-road excursions are a popular choice. These tours are perfect for exploring the vast sand dunes and rocky desert terrain. You'll be able to reach remote oases, see ancient ruins, and enjoy the thrill of driving through the desert. Experienced drivers and guides are available to ensure a safe yet exhilarating adventure.

3. **Star Gazing and Overnight Camping**
   - The desert offers some of the clearest skies in the world, making it a prime location for star gazing. Many desert excursions near Tunis include overnight camping under the stars. You'll stay in a traditional Berber-style tent, enjoy a campfire meal, and be mesmerized by the sight of the stars above.

The serenity of the desert night is a unique experience that many travelers cherish.
4. **Cultural Experiences and Festivals**
    - Desert excursions near Tunis offer the chance to immerse yourself in traditional Berber culture. You can visit local nomadic communities, learn about their way of life, and discover traditional crafts such as carpet weaving and pottery making. If you happen to visit during the annual **Festival of the Sahara** in Douz, you can enjoy music, dance, camel races, and other cultural celebrations.

Essential Tips for Desert Excursions Near Tunis

- **Best Time to Visit**: The desert can get extremely hot, especially in the summer months, so the best time for desert excursions is during the cooler months, from October to April. The winter months (December to February) offer mild temperatures, making for a more comfortable adventure.
- **What to Wear**:
    - **Light, breathable clothing**: Desert temperatures can vary drastically from day to night, so wear lightweight, loose-fitting clothes that can protect you from the sun but also allow for cooling.
    - **Sun protection**: Bring a wide-brimmed hat, sunglasses, and sunscreen to protect yourself from the intense desert sun.

- o **Sturdy footwear**: If you're planning to hike or trek, wear sturdy boots suitable for sand and rocky terrain.
- o **Layered clothing**: Nights in the desert can get cold, so bring warm clothing if you're planning to stay overnight.
- **Hydration**: The desert environment is dry, and you may experience dehydration quickly. Be sure to drink plenty of water, especially if you're participating in activities like camel trekking or 4x4 tours.
- **Respect the Environment**: Desert ecosystems are fragile. Avoid disturbing the wildlife, and stay on marked trails or paths to prevent damaging the natural habitat.

DAY TRIPS AND EXCURSIONS FROM TUNIS

Tunis is perfectly situated for exploring several remarkable destinations within a few hours' drive. If you're interested in ancient ruins, beautiful beaches, or picturesque towns, there are many exciting day trips and excursions that will enrich your travel experience. Here are some of the most popular options, each offering its own unique charm and history.

Dougga

Dougga, located in the northwestern part of Tunisia, is one of the most impressive and well-preserved Roman archaeological sites in North Africa. This ancient Roman town, once called "Thugga," dates back to the 2nd century BC and was a thriving city during Roman times. Today, it is a UNESCO World Heritage site, offering visitors a glimpse into the grandeur and architectural brilliance of ancient Rome. Its rich history, beautiful surroundings, and impressive ruins make it a must-see for history enthusiasts and travelers seeking to explore Tunisia's ancient past.

Top Highlights

- **Roman Theater:** The Roman Theater in Dougga is one of the most iconic structures in the site. It could accommodate up to 3,500 spectators and is beautifully situated on a hill with stunning views of the surrounding countryside. The theater is still in relatively good condition and is often used for local cultural events, providing a rare chance to experience a performance in such a historically significant setting.

- **Capitoline Temple:** Dedicated to the Roman gods Jupiter, Juno, and Minerva, the Capitolium or Capitoline Temple is another highlight of Dougga. It stands majestically on a raised platform and offers a panoramic view of the ancient city. The temple's impressive columns and intricate carvings demonstrate the grandeur of Roman religious architecture.
- **Triumphal Arch of Septimius Severus:** This arch was constructed in honor of Emperor Septimius Severus, a native of North Africa who became the Roman Emperor. The arch is adorned with beautiful carvings depicting significant moments from his reign and serves as a testament to his power and influence.
- **The Forum:** The Forum is the central square of the city, where public life once thrived. It's surrounded by the remains of various temples, basilicas, and other significant buildings. Visitors can walk through the ruins and imagine the bustling life that once filled this area with political and social activity.
- **Private Villas and Mosaics:** Dougga is home to several well-preserved private villas, with intricate mosaics that give insight into the daily lives of its residents. These mosaics are famous for their vivid depictions of mythological scenes, animals, and daily activities, showcasing the artistic talent of the period.
- **Roman Baths:** The site also includes the remains of Roman baths, which were an important aspect of Roman social life. These baths feature large pools, hot rooms, and changing areas, and visiting them offers a unique glimpse into the leisure practices of ancient Romans.

Travel Tips

- **Getting There**: Dougga is located about 2.5 hours by car from Tunis. To get there, you can either rent a car, take a guided tour, or use public transportation. Public transport is less frequent, so having a car will allow you more flexibility.
- **What to Bring**: Comfortable walking shoes are essential, as the site involves a fair amount of walking on uneven terrain. Bring a hat, sunscreen, and water to stay hydrated, especially during the warmer months. A camera is also a must to capture the stunning ruins and panoramic views.
- **Best Time to Visit**: The best time to visit Dougga is during the cooler months, from October to April. Summer temperatures can be intense, so visiting during spring or fall will make for a more comfortable and enjoyable experience. Early morning or late afternoon visits also provide softer lighting for photography.
- **Guides**: While Dougga can be explored independently, hiring a local guide is highly recommended. A guide can provide historical context and explain the significance of the various ruins, which can enhance your understanding of the site.
- **Duration of Visit**: Plan to spend around 2 to 3 hours exploring Dougga. The site is large, and there's plenty to see, so take your time to fully appreciate the archaeological wonders.

Cap Bon Peninsula

Located just 1.5 hours from Tunis, the Cap Bon Peninsula offers an idyllic escape from the bustling city, combining beautiful beaches, vibrant coastal towns, and picturesque landscapes. This region, often referred to as the "garden of Tunisia," is famous for its pleasant climate, fertile soil, and Mediterranean charm. Whether you're seeking relaxation on sandy shores, cultural exploration in traditional towns, or an authentic taste of Tunisia's winemaking heritage, Cap Bon is the perfect destination for a day trip.

Top Highlights

- **Hammamet:** Known for its beautiful beaches, Hammamet is one of Tunisia's most popular coastal destinations. The town has a charming old Medina, with narrow, winding streets filled with artisan shops and cafes. The **Kasbah of Hammamet**, perched above the town, offers spectacular views of the Mediterranean Sea and the surrounding area. Hammamet is also home to several luxurious resorts, making it a great spot for relaxation and rejuvenation.
    - **Best Activities**: Strolling through the Medina, visiting the Kasbah, relaxing on Hammamet Beach, and enjoying water sports such as jet-skiing and windsurfing.
    - **Dining**: Don't miss the chance to sample local seafood at one of the town's beachfront restaurants.
- **Nabeul:** Nabeul is the heart of the Cap Bon Peninsula and is renowned for its pottery. The town's markets are filled with brightly colored ceramic goods, and it's a great place to shop for souvenirs. Nabeul also has a lively weekly market (souq), where you can find everything from local spices to fresh produce.
    - **Best Activities**: Shopping at the pottery souk, exploring the local markets, and visiting the **Nabeul**

> **Archaeological Museum** to learn about the region's history.
> - **Dining**: Nabeul is famous for its traditional Tunisian cuisine. Try a local dish such as **brik**, a pastry filled with egg, tuna, and capers.

- **The Vineyards of Cap Bon:** Cap Bon is one of Tunisia's key wine-producing regions, and visitors can tour local vineyards to learn about traditional winemaking techniques. The **Muscat of Alexandria** is a standout variety produced in this area, and you can sample various wines while learning about Tunisia's ancient winemaking heritage.
  - **Best Activities**: Wine tasting at local vineyards, touring the cellars, and learning about Tunisia's winemaking history.
  - **Recommended Vineyards**: **Domaine Neferis** and **Domaine Bou Argoub** are among the region's top wine estates, offering tours and tastings.
- **Korba:** Korba is a quieter town on the Cap Bon Peninsula, perfect for those looking to escape the crowds. It is known for its beautiful sandy beaches and peaceful atmosphere. The area is ideal for a relaxing day by the sea, enjoying the natural beauty and Mediterranean views.
  - **Best Activities**: Spending a day on the beach, enjoying fresh seafood at a seaside restaurant, and exploring the small town's charming streets.
  - **Dining**: Enjoy local seafood specialties at one of Korba's beachside eateries.
- **Kelibia:** Kelibia, located on the northeastern tip of the Cap Bon Peninsula, is famous for its stunning beaches and the **Fort of Kelibia**, a historic fortress offering panoramic views of the sea. The fort dates back to the 16th century

and provides a fascinating glimpse into the region's strategic history.
  - **Best Activities**: Visiting the Fort of Kelibia, enjoying the pristine beaches, and exploring the charming town.

Travel Tips

- **Getting There**: The Cap Bon Peninsula is just a 1.5-hour drive from Tunis, making it a convenient day trip. Renting a car is the most efficient way to explore the area, though there are also guided tours available.
- **What to Bring**: For a beach day, pack swimwear, sunscreen, a hat, and a beach towel. If you plan to visit vineyards, bring a light jacket for cooler evenings, as well as comfortable walking shoes.
- **Best Time to Visit**: The best time to visit the Cap Bon Peninsula is during the spring and fall when temperatures are pleasant and the landscape is lush. The summer months can be hot, but the region's beaches provide a perfect escape.
- **Guided Tours**: While it's easy to explore the peninsula independently, guided tours can enhance your experience, especially when visiting vineyards or the historical sites in Hammamet and Kelibia.
- **Duration of Visit**: For a comprehensive experience, plan on spending a full day exploring the Cap Bon Peninsula. If you want to focus on just one or two towns, half a day is sufficient.

El Jem

El Jem, located in central Tunisia, is one of the most iconic Roman archaeological sites in the Mediterranean. Known for its colossal amphitheater, it provides a fascinating insight into the grandeur and engineering prowess of the ancient Roman Empire. This UNESCO World Heritage site was once a major city in Roman Africa, thriving during the 3rd century AD. Today, it stands as a powerful reminder of the region's historical significance and offers visitors a deep dive into Roman architecture and culture.

Top Highlights

- **El Jem Amphitheater:** The El Jem Amphitheater is the crown jewel of the site and one of the best-preserved Roman arenas in the world. With a capacity of around 35,000 spectators, it is the third-largest amphitheater in the Roman Empire, following the Colosseum in Rome and the amphitheater in Capua. The structure is remarkably intact, with its impressive outer walls still standing tall, and the inner arena is well-preserved. Visitors can walk through the arena, explore the underground chambers that housed gladiators and animals, and climb to the upper tiers for a panoramic view of the surrounding landscape. The amphitheater is a must-see for anyone interested in Roman history, architecture, and the brutal spectacles that once took place here.
- **The El Jem Museum:** Located near the amphitheater, the El Jem Museum offers a wealth of information about the region's Roman past. The museum houses a vast collection of Roman mosaics, statues, and artifacts that were unearthed in El Jem and surrounding areas. Many of these

items depict daily life, mythological scenes, and even gladiatorial contests, providing visitors with a deeper understanding of the cultural and social dynamics of Roman Africa. The museum is small but informative, and it offers an excellent opportunity to learn more about the ancient city's history.
- **The Arch of Carthage:** While the El Jem amphitheater is the main attraction, the city itself once contained many other significant Roman structures, including the Arch of Carthage. Though not as well-preserved, this monument once commemorated the victory of the Roman forces over Carthage. It provides a glimpse into the celebratory architecture of the time and is worth a brief visit if you're in the area.

Travel Tips

- **Getting There**: El Jem is located about 2.5 hours by car from Tunis. It can be accessed by car, and there are several tour companies offering day trips from Tunis. Public transportation options, such as buses or trains, are also available but may be less convenient.
- **What to Bring**: Comfortable walking shoes are essential for exploring the amphitheater and the surrounding site. Don't forget sunscreen, a hat, and plenty of water, especially in the warmer months. A camera is also recommended to capture the impressive structures and views.
- **Best Time to Visit**: To avoid the heat of the summer, it's best to visit El Jem during the cooler months, between October and April. The site can get quite hot in the

summer, so early morning or late afternoon visits are recommended during this period.
- **Duration of Visit**: Plan to spend 2 to 3 hours at El Jem, which will give you enough time to explore the amphitheater, visit the museum, and take in the surrounding area.

Zaghouan

Zaghouan, a historic town located about 1.5 hours from Tunis, is known for its well-preserved Roman waterworks and its proximity to Mount Zaghouan. The town played a crucial role in providing water to the ancient city of Carthage, and visitors can still see the remains of the sophisticated water systems that once carried water over great distances. Zaghouan also boasts stunning natural landscapes, including waterfalls and mountain views, making it an excellent destination for both history and nature lovers.

Top Highlights

- **Roman Aqueduct:** The most impressive feature of Zaghouan is its Roman aqueduct, which was used to transport water from the town's springs to Carthage. The aqueduct is one of the most remarkable engineering feats of the Roman Empire in North Africa, and parts of it are still visible today. The water was channeled through a series of stone arches and tunnels that spanned across the landscape. Walking along parts of the aqueduct gives visitors a sense of how advanced Roman engineering was, and the views of the surrounding countryside are spectacular.
- **Temple of Water (Temple of the Nymphs):** This ancient Roman temple is dedicated to the nymphs and the Roman goddess of water, which highlights the importance of water

in Roman society. The temple is a symbol of the connection between religion and the vital resource of water. While much of the temple is in ruins, the remaining structure provides a sense of the grandiosity that would have once characterized the site. The location offers a peaceful setting with stunning views of the surrounding hills.
- **Mount Zaghouan:** For nature lovers, a visit to Mount Zaghouan is a must. The mountain is part of the Tell Atlas range and offers beautiful hiking trails that take visitors through lush forests, rocky outcrops, and scenic viewpoints. Hiking to the summit provides panoramic views of the surrounding area, including the town of Zaghouan and the far-reaching Mediterranean coast. The mountain is home to diverse flora and fauna, making it a great spot for nature walks and bird watching.
- **Zaghouan Waterfalls:** Situated near the base of Mount Zaghouan, the waterfalls are a natural attraction that draws visitors looking to enjoy the tranquility of nature. The falls are particularly beautiful in the spring when the water flow is at its peak. The area surrounding the falls is a peaceful spot to relax and enjoy the fresh mountain air.

Travel Tips

- **Getting There**: Zaghouan is approximately 1.5 hours by car from Tunis. Renting a car is the most convenient option, but there are also guided tours available that include transportation. The town can also be reached by bus, but it might be less comfortable and take longer.
- **What to Bring**: Comfortable shoes for walking, especially if you plan on hiking around the aqueduct or climbing

Mount Zaghouan. Bring sunscreen, a hat, and water, as temperatures can get quite high in the summer. If you plan to visit the waterfalls or hike, pack a light jacket, especially in the cooler months.

- **Best Time to Visit**: The best time to visit Zaghouan is during the spring and fall when the weather is moderate, and hiking is most enjoyable. Summer can be hot, so it's advisable to visit early in the morning or later in the afternoon.
- **Duration of Visit**: A visit to Zaghouan can typically take about 3 to 4 hours, depending on whether you are hiking, exploring the aqueduct, or visiting the waterfalls. If you wish to enjoy a full day of hiking and sightseeing, you might want to allocate additional time for a leisurely exploration of the area.

Kairouan

Kairouan, located about two hours from Tunis, is one of Tunisia's most historically and culturally significant cities. It is considered the fourth holiest city in Islam, after Mecca, Medina, and Jerusalem, and is a UNESCO World Heritage site. Founded in the 7th century, Kairouan became an important center for Islamic scholarship, culture, and architecture. The city's rich history is visible in its many mosques, medinas, and monuments, making it an essential destination for anyone interested in Islamic heritage.

Top Highlights

- **Great Mosque of Kairouan (Mosque of Uqba):** The Great Mosque of Kairouan, also known as the Mosque of Uqba, is one of the oldest and most important mosques in the Muslim world. Built in the 9th century, the mosque's architecture is a stunning example of early Islamic design. The massive courtyard, intricately designed prayer hall, and impressive minaret make it a must-see. The mosque is an active place of worship, so visitors should be respectful of prayer times. The mosque also houses a library with rare Islamic texts, making it an important scholarly site.

- **The Medina of Kairouan:** Kairouan's Medina is a maze of narrow, winding streets lined with traditional shops, artisan workshops, and vibrant markets. Visitors can explore the medina and shop for local handicrafts, including carpets, pottery, and textiles. The Medina is also home to many historic buildings, including schools (madrasas) and mausoleums, offering a glimpse into the city's rich past. The area has a charming, timeless feel, with much of its architecture dating back to the medieval Islamic period.
- **Aghlabid Basins:** The Aghlabid Basins, also known as the Aghlabid Pools, are a fascinating feat of ancient engineering. These massive water reservoirs were built by the Aghlabid dynasty in the 9th century to supply Kairouan with water. The basins are still in remarkable condition, and visitors can explore them to appreciate the scale of this monumental water management project. The site is peaceful and offers an opportunity to learn more about the technical ingenuity of the Aghlabids.
- **Barber's Tomb (Mausoleum of Sidi Sahab):** The Mausoleum of Sidi Sahab, also known as the Barber's Tomb, is one of the most revered sites in Kairouan. It is believed to be the burial place of a companion of the Prophet Muhammad, who was said to be the prophet's barber. The mausoleum is beautifully decorated with tiles

and intricate mosaics, reflecting the Islamic architectural style. The peaceful ambiance and the spiritual significance of the site make it a must-visit for those interested in Islamic history.
- **Kairouan's Historic Mosques and Madrasas:** In addition to the Great Mosque, Kairouan is home to several other historic mosques and madrasas (Islamic schools). The **Mosque of the Three Doors**, **Zitouna Mosque**, and **Sidi Jabeer Mosque** are just a few examples of the beautiful religious buildings that dot the city. These structures showcase a range of architectural styles, from early Islamic designs to later, more intricate styles, and each offers insights into the religious and cultural life of Kairouan's inhabitants.

Travel Tips

- **Getting There**: Kairouan is easily accessible from Tunis by car, taking approximately 2 hours. There are also buses and trains available, though a private car or guided tour offers more flexibility, especially for visiting the city's key attractions.
- **What to Bring**: Kairouan is a relatively conservative city, so it's important to dress modestly, especially when visiting religious sites. Comfortable walking shoes are essential for exploring the medina's narrow streets. A hat and sunscreen are also recommended, as temperatures can rise, especially in the summer.
- **Best Time to Visit**: The best time to visit Kairouan is in the cooler months, from October to April, when the weather is more comfortable for walking and exploring. Summer can

be extremely hot, so early morning or late afternoon visits are recommended during these months.
- **Duration of Visit**: A visit to Kairouan can be done in one day, but to fully explore the city's many mosques, medinas, and historical sites, plan on spending a full day or even longer if you want to dive deep into the city's history and culture.

Day trips from Tunis offer an incredible opportunity to explore the diverse cultural, historical, and natural treasures of Tunisia. From the well-preserved Roman ruins of **Dougga** and **El Jem**, to the ancient waterworks in **Zaghouan** and the spiritual heart of **Kairouan**, each destination provides a unique glimpse into the country's rich heritage. Whether you're interested in archaeological sites, religious landmarks, or scenic landscapes, these excursions are perfect for travelers looking to enhance their Tunisian experience beyond the capital. With convenient access by car or organized tours, these day trips are an essential part of any itinerary, offering both relaxation and adventure for every type of traveler.

DINING IN TUNIS

Tunis offers a vibrant and flavorful culinary scene, blending traditional Tunisian dishes with Mediterranean and Middle Eastern influences. From street food to fine dining, the city provides a rich gastronomic experience for travelers. Here's an essential guide to dining in Tunis:

Must-Try Tunisian Dishes

Tunisian cuisine is a delightful mix of Mediterranean flavors, Arabic influences, and Berber traditions. Whether you're enjoying a home-cooked meal or dining out at a local restaurant, these iconic dishes are a must-try for any traveler. Below is an expanded list of essential Tunisian dishes that offer an authentic taste of the country's rich culinary heritage.

Couscous

Couscous is Tunisia's national dish, and you will find it served in various forms across the country. Made from steamed semolina wheat, couscous is a versatile dish that can be paired with different types of meats, fish, and vegetables.

- **Couscous with Lamb or Beef:** A classic Tunisian version often includes tender lamb or beef cooked in a rich tomato-based sauce, flavored with spices like cumin, coriander, and saffron.
- **Couscous with Fish (Couscous with Chermoula):** Coastal regions favor seafood couscous, typically served

with fish such as tuna or cod, marinated in a vibrant chermoula sauce (a mixture of garlic, parsley, and spices).
- **Vegetable Couscous:** For vegetarians, couscous served with a mix of roasted vegetables, such as carrots, zucchini, and squash, is a popular choice.

Tip: Couscous is often served during communal gatherings, making it a perfect dish to try in a traditional Tunisian home.

Brik

A quintessential Tunisian appetizer, **Brik** is a deep-fried pastry stuffed with various fillings. The most common version is filled with a raw egg, tuna, and capers, and sometimes includes harissa (a spicy paste made from chilies, garlic, and olive oil). The crispy exterior contrasts beautifully with the gooey, runny egg inside, creating a delightful textural experience.

- **Brik with Egg:** The traditional version, with a whole egg in the center that cooks perfectly as the brik is fried.
- **Brik with Meat:** Some variations include minced lamb or chicken, combined with vegetables or olives for added flavor.

Tip: Brik is often served with a fresh squeeze of lemon, enhancing its savory flavor.

Lablabi

Lablabi is a hearty, comforting chickpea soup that's perfect for cooler days or as a filling lunch. This dish consists of a spiced chickpea broth, typically flavored with garlic, cumin, and coriander, and served with torn pieces of stale bread, which absorb the rich broth. Often topped with a poached egg and a dollop of harissa, lablabi is a deeply satisfying dish.

- **Toppings:** Lablabi is customizable, with options to add olives, tuna, or even lamb to enhance the flavor profile.
- **Spices:** The key to a good lablabi is the generous use of cumin and coriander, which give it a warm, aromatic flavor.

Tip: For an authentic experience, enjoy lablabi at a local market stall, where it's often served fresh and piping hot.

Harissa

Harissa is Tunisia's signature chili paste and is used as a condiment in nearly every meal. Made from roasted red peppers, garlic, coriander seeds, and caraway, it adds a spicy kick to dishes like couscous, grilled meats, and soups.

- **Homemade Harissa:** Many Tunisian families make their own harissa, which has a more intense flavor than store-bought versions.
- **Harissa with Olive Oil:** It's common to mix harissa with olive oil to create a smooth, spreadable paste that can be enjoyed with bread.

Tip: If you're a fan of spice, make sure to ask for extra harissa when ordering any dish—it's a must-have accompaniment!

Ojja

Ojja is a spicy, flavorful tomato-based stew that can include eggs, sausages, or seafood. The dish is simmered with onions, garlic, tomatoes, and a mix of spices, creating a thick and aromatic base.

- **Ojja with Merguez Sausage:** A popular variation includes **merguez** sausages (spicy lamb sausages) that are added to the stew, soaking up the rich flavors.
- **Ojja with Eggs:** The eggs are cracked directly into the stew just before serving, cooking gently in the bubbling sauce, which gives the dish a deliciously creamy texture.

Tip: Ojja is often served with fresh bread to mop up the flavorful sauce, making it a perfect dish for sharing.

Mechouia Salad

Salad Mechouia is a roasted vegetable salad that's a staple of Tunisian cuisine, typically served as a side dish or appetizer. The vegetables—usually tomatoes, peppers, onions, and eggplant—are roasted until soft and charred, then peeled and chopped. The salad is dressed with olive oil, garlic, and a generous amount of harissa, giving it a smoky, spicy flavor.

- **Optional Additions:** Some versions of mechouia include hard-boiled eggs or tuna, making it a more substantial dish.
- **Fresh and Tangy:** A squeeze of lemon juice often brightens up the salad, balancing the smoky, spicy elements.

Tip: Mechouia can be served warm or cold and is especially popular during the summer months when the ingredients are at their freshest.

Makroud

Makroud is a sweet, semolina-based pastry that's often enjoyed as a dessert or snack. The dough is typically filled with dates, almonds, or figs and then deep-fried until golden and crispy. The pastry is then soaked in honey, giving it a sweet, sticky finish.

- **Makroud with Dates:** The classic filling, combining the rich, sweet flavor of dates with the nuttiness of almonds.
- **Makroud with Syrup:** Often drizzled with rose or orange blossom syrup to add floral undertones.

Tip: Makroud is best enjoyed with a cup of traditional Tunisian mint tea, balancing the sweetness of the pastry.

Tajine

In Tunisia, **tajine** refers to a type of casserole rather than the slow-cooked stews common in other parts of North Africa. Tunisian tajine is made with a variety of ingredients, from vegetables to meats, and is held together with a mixture of eggs and spices that form a soft, custard-like texture when baked.

- **Tajine with Lamb or Chicken:** Meat is often used as the main protein in tajine, providing a savory base for the dish.
- **Tajine with Vegetables:** A great option for vegetarians, made with seasonal vegetables like carrots, zucchini, and potatoes, all mixed with eggs and seasoned with aromatic herbs.

Tip: This dish is often served at family gatherings or as a special meal for guests, making it an ideal choice for those looking to experience authentic Tunisian hospitality.

Fritures de Poisson (Fried Fish)

Tunis, with its proximity to the Mediterranean Sea, is known for fresh seafood. **Fried fish** is a popular dish, especially along the coast. Typically served with a side of fried potatoes or a fresh salad, the fish is lightly seasoned and fried until crispy.

- **Fried Squid and Fish:** Many places serve a mix of fish, squid, and shrimp, all deep-fried to perfection.
- **Lemon and Harissa:** A squeeze of lemon and a side of harissa are essential to complement the delicate flavor of the fried seafood.

Tip: Try this dish at a seaside restaurant for the freshest seafood experience.

Shorba

Shorba is a flavorful soup that's popular in Tunisia, especially during Ramadan. Made with lamb, chicken, or vegetables, this soup is spiced with turmeric, coriander, and sometimes saffron, giving it a fragrant, rich broth. Shorba is often served as a starter before a main meal.

- **Shorba with Lamb:** A hearty version made with tender lamb pieces, ideal for a comforting meal.
- **Vegetable Shorba:** For those preferring a lighter option, a vegetable-based version is equally satisfying.

Tip: Shorba is often eaten with **khobz**, a traditional Tunisian bread that soaks up the flavorful broth.

Best Restaurants for Tunisian Cuisine

Tunis is a culinary paradise for those eager to dive into authentic Tunisian flavors. From traditional settings in the Medina to contemporary spots blending old and new, these restaurants deliver exceptional Tunisian cuisine experiences:

Dar El Jeld

Located in the heart of the Medina, **Dar El Jeld** is renowned for its elegant atmosphere and dedication to preserving traditional Tunisian flavors. Set in a beautifully restored historic house, the restaurant offers a luxurious dining experience.

- **Specialties:** Lamb couscous, brik à l'œuf, and mechouia salad.
- **Ambiance:** Upscale, intimate, and adorned with intricate tilework and arches that reflect the city's architectural heritage.
- **Tip:** Reservations are recommended, especially for dinner, as this is one of the most sought-after dining spots in Tunis.

Restaurant El Ali

A cultural haven near the Zitouna Mosque, **Restaurant El Ali** combines authentic cuisine with an artistic vibe. The rooftop dining area offers stunning views of the Medina, enhancing the dining experience.

- **Specialties:** Ojja with merguez, seafood couscous, and refreshing mint tea.
- **Ambiance:** Warm, welcoming, and ideal for immersing yourself in Tunisian culture.

- **Tip:** Visit during lunch hours to enjoy the sunlight streaming into the dining area and a calmer atmosphere.

Chez Slah

A favorite among locals and visitors, **Chez Slah** is a hidden gem known for its outstanding seafood and well-prepared Tunisian classics.

- **Specialties:** Grilled fish, seafood pasta, and lamb tagine.
- **Ambiance:** Casual yet charming, with a focus on fresh ingredients and authentic flavors.
- **Tip:** Arrive early or book ahead, as the restaurant has limited seating and is very popular.

Dar Zarrouk

Situated in the picturesque village of Sidi Bou Said, **Dar Zarrouk** offers breathtaking views of the Mediterranean alongside its fine Tunisian menu.

- **Specialties:** Grilled octopus, lamb mechoui (roast lamb), and saffron-infused couscous.
- **Ambiance:** Elegant and romantic, perfect for a special evening.
- **Tip:** Try to reserve a table on the terrace to enjoy the sea breeze and stunning vistas.

Fondouk El Attarine

Nestled in a historic caravanserai in the Medina, **Fondouk El Attarine** provides an authentic Tunisian dining experience with a modern twist.

- **Specialties:** Brik with shrimp, lamb with prunes, and makroud for dessert.
- **Ambiance:** Traditional yet chic, with an artistic setting showcasing local craftsmanship.
- **Tip:** Pair your meal with a local wine for a complete Tunisian culinary journey.

International Dining Options

Tunis offers an impressive range of international cuisine, catering to travelers seeking flavors from around the globe. From Italian trattorias to Asian fusion, the city's diverse dining scene guarantees something for everyone.

Le Grand Café du Théâtre

Located on Avenue Habib Bourguiba, **Le Grand Café du Théâtre** is a sophisticated spot for French-inspired cuisine.

- **Specialties:** Duck confit, steak frites, and crème brûlée.
- **Ambiance:** Chic and Parisian, with indoor and outdoor seating perfect for people-watching.
- **Tip:** Ideal for a leisurely brunch or pre-theater dinner.

La Closerie

For a Mediterranean fine-dining experience, **La Closerie** in La Marsa is a must-visit. This upscale restaurant serves a mix of Italian, French, and Tunisian dishes.

- **Specialties:** Risotto with seafood, grilled lamb chops, and tiramisu.

- **Ambiance:** Sophisticated and modern, with a garden terrace for al fresco dining.
- **Tip:** Perfect for romantic dinners or special celebrations.

Asian Taste

If you're craving Asian flavors, **Asian Taste** in Berges du Lac offers a menu inspired by Chinese, Japanese, and Thai cuisines.

- **Specialties:** Sushi platters, pad Thai, and Peking duck.
- **Ambiance:** Contemporary and vibrant, ideal for both casual and formal meals.
- **Tip:** Their sushi is highly recommended, as it features fresh, locally sourced seafood.

La Salle à Manger

This stylish French bistro in La Marsa delivers authentic French cuisine with a Tunisian touch.

- **Specialties:** Coq au vin, ratatouille, and profiteroles.
- **Ambiance:** Cozy and intimate, with rustic-chic decor.
- **Tip:** Reserve a table in advance, as it's a favorite among expatriates and locals alike.

Villa Didon

Located in Carthage, **Villa Didon** offers stunning views of the ancient ruins and a menu combining Mediterranean and modern global flavors.

- **Specialties:** Lobster ravioli, seared tuna, and chocolate fondant.

- **Ambiance:** Sleek and contemporary, with panoramic views from its glass-walled dining room.
- **Tip:** Visit at sunset for an unforgettable dining experience.

Pizzeria Taormina

For Italian food lovers, **Pizzeria Taormina** in Tunis provides an authentic Italian dining experience.

- **Specialties:** Wood-fired pizzas, creamy carbonara, and tiramisu.
- **Ambiance:** Casual and family-friendly, with a focus on comfort and quality.
- **Tip:** Their quattro formaggi pizza is a standout dish.

Yüka

A trendy fusion restaurant in Gammarth, **Yüka** specializes in global dishes with a creative twist.

- **Specialties:** Fusion sushi, gourmet burgers, and artisan cocktails.
- **Ambiance:** Vibrant and energetic, with live music on certain evenings.
- **Tip:** Make it a night out by enjoying their live entertainment while dining.

Street Food in Tunis

Exploring street food in Tunis is a feast for the senses. These vibrant hubs offer a glimpse into the everyday life of Tunisians and are perfect for sampling authentic dishes, discovering fresh produce, and soaking in the city's energetic atmosphere.

Must-Try Street Foods

Tunisian street food is packed with bold flavors, combining fresh ingredients and a variety of spices. Here are some popular options:

- **Bambalouni:** A Tunisian doughnut made from a yeast-based dough, deep-fried until golden, and sprinkled with sugar. It's a favorite sweet treat, often enjoyed fresh and warm.
- **Kafteji:** A mix of fried vegetables like peppers, tomatoes, and potatoes, often topped with a fried egg or served with bread. This hearty dish is a local favorite for a quick lunch.
- **Mloukhia Sandwiches:** A sandwich filled with a thick, dark stew made from dried jute leaves, beef, and spices. It's rich, savory, and a must-try for adventurous eaters.
- **Lablabi:** A warm and comforting chickpea soup served from street stalls, often garnished with harissa, olive oil, and a soft-boiled egg. It's a great pick-me-up after a long day of exploring.
- **Ojja Tacos:** A street-friendly version of the traditional spicy egg and sausage stew, served wrapped in flatbread for convenience.

Street Food Tips

- **Freshness:** Opt for stalls with high turnover to ensure the food is freshly prepared.
- **Timing:** Visit during peak hours for the best selection and lively atmosphere.
- **Hygiene:** Choose vendors with clean preparation areas and properly displayed food.

Cafés and Coffee Culture in Tunis

Cafés are an integral part of Tunisian culture, serving as places to unwind, socialize, or enjoy a moment of solitude. Tunis boasts a variety of cafés, from historic establishments to modern coffeehouses, where you can indulge in Tunisian coffee, tea, and pastries.

Traditional Tunisian Coffee

- **Café Turk (Turkish Coffee):** Made in a traditional **dallah** (coffee pot) and served in small cups, Tunisian coffee is strong, aromatic, and often spiced with cardamom.
- **Café Direct (Espresso):** Italian influence has popularized espresso-style coffee, often served with a side of water.

Tip: Tunisian coffee is usually unsweetened; add sugar according to your taste.

Mint Tea and Other Favorites

Mint tea is a staple of Tunisian café culture, typically served in small glasses and sweetened generously. Variations include:

- **Tea with Pine Nuts:** A luxurious version garnished with floating pine nuts.
- **Rosemary Tea:** Infused with fresh rosemary for a unique herbal flavor.

Tip: Order tea during the late afternoon for a quintessential Tunisian experience.

Iconic Cafés to Visit

Tunis is home to a variety of cafés, each with its own charm and offerings.

- **Café Sidi Bou Said (Café des Nattes):** Located in the picturesque village of Sidi Bou Said, this café is famous for its mint tea, Turkish coffee, and traditional ambiance. Sit on the colorful cushions and enjoy views of the Mediterranean.
- **Café Culturel Liber'Thé:** A trendy spot in the city center offering a mix of traditional Tunisian drinks and contemporary coffee styles. It's a great place for creative minds and book lovers.
- **Café Panorama:** As the name suggests, this café offers panoramic views of Tunis from its rooftop terrace. Enjoy a cup of coffee while watching the city skyline at sunset.
- **Café Mrabet:** Situated in the Medina, this historic café serves as a cultural landmark. It's an excellent spot to relax after shopping and enjoy a cup of tea with traditional Tunisian sweets.

Modern Coffeehouses

For travelers seeking international coffee styles or a cozy place to work, Tunis also has a growing number of modern coffee shops.

- **The Factory Café:** Known for its laid-back atmosphere and variety of coffee blends, it's a favorite among young Tunisians.
- **La Marsa Coffee Roasters:** Located in La Marsa, this café specializes in artisanal coffee, offering pour-over and cold brew options.

- **Latino Coffee:** A fusion café serving lattes, cappuccinos, and light snacks in a trendy setting.

Café Tips

- **Etiquette:** Tunisians often linger over their drinks, so feel free to take your time and enjoy the ambiance.
- **Timing:** Late afternoons and evenings are the best times to visit cafés, as they become lively social hubs.
- **Sweets Pairing:** Order traditional pastries like **makroud** or **bambalouni** with your drink for the full experience.

Vegetarian and Vegan Dining in Tunis

Tunis is increasingly accommodating to vegetarian and vegan travelers, although traditional Tunisian cuisine often features meat or fish. With a little exploration, you'll find plenty of plant-based options that highlight the region's fresh produce, spices, and creativity.

Vegetarian-Friendly Tunisian Dishes

- **Brik:** Typically stuffed with egg and herbs, this crispy pastry can be customized with vegetable fillings.
- **Ojja:** A hearty tomato-based stew, often served with vegetables or eggs. Ask for a meat-free version.
- **Couscous with Vegetables:** A popular dish featuring steamed semolina, seasonal vegetables, and aromatic spices.
- **Mechouia Salad:** A smoky blend of grilled peppers, tomatoes, and olive oil, served as a starter or side dish.
- **Lablabi:** While traditionally served with eggs, this chickpea soup can easily be adapted for vegans.

Vegan-Friendly Options

- **Harissa Platters:** Many restaurants serve harissa (a spicy chili paste) with bread and olives as a starter, which is naturally vegan.
- **Fresh Fruit and Nuts:** Street vendors and markets offer seasonal fruit and locally grown almonds, dates, and pistachios.
- **Tabbouleh:** A refreshing salad made with parsley, tomatoes, and bulgur, commonly found in Mediterranean-inspired eateries.
- **Roasted Vegetables:** Found in many casual dining spots and markets, often served with tahini or olive oil.

Tip: Mention dietary preferences to the staff, as many dishes can be adjusted to suit vegan or vegetarian needs.

Vegetarian and Vegan-Friendly Restaurants

- **La Cuisine Tunisienne:** Offers a variety of vegetarian couscous and mezze platters.
- **Bio Gourmet:** A health-conscious café with a focus on organic, plant-based options, including salads and smoothies.
- **Beit El-Fel:** This casual eatery in Sidi Bou Said serves delicious vegetarian Tunisian dishes.
- **Green Bar:** Located in La Marsa, it specializes in vegan-friendly wraps, juices, and desserts.

Dining Etiquette and Tips

Understanding Tunisian dining customs ensures a pleasant and respectful experience:

1. **Meal Times:** Lunch is the main meal, often served between 1:00 PM and 3:00 PM, while dinner is lighter and later, starting around 8:00 PM.
2. **Use of Hands:** Bread is often used as a utensil to scoop food. When using hands, always use your right hand, as it's considered polite.
3. **Sharing:** Tunisian meals are often communal. Wait for the host to begin eating and offer dishes before serving yourself.
4. **Pace:** Meals are leisurely and social affairs. Take your time to enjoy the food and conversation.
5. **Tipping:** While not mandatory, a tip of 10% is appreciated in most restaurants. For exceptional service, feel free to leave more.

Useful Websites and Resources for Dining in Tunis

To enhance your dining experiences in Tunis, these websites and resources provide valuable insights into local restaurants, street food, and culinary culture. They are helpful for both planning ahead and making on-the-go decisions.

1. TripAdvisor

Website: www.tripadvisor.com
Overview:

- Offers detailed reviews, ratings, and photos of restaurants in Tunis.
- Features lists of top-rated eateries for Tunisian cuisine, international dining, and hidden gems.
Best For: Finding highly-rated restaurants and authentic local dining spots.

2. The Fork (La Fourchette)

Website: www.thefork.com
Overview:

- Allows reservations at some of the best restaurants in Tunis.
- Provides promotions, menus, and user reviews.
  Best For: Booking a table at upscale and popular dining establishments in advance.

3. Zomato

Website: www.zomato.com
Overview:

- Features menus, contact information, and user-generated reviews.
- Categorizes eateries based on cuisine, price range, and ambiance.
  Best For: Exploring dining options filtered by preferences, such as vegetarian or vegan-friendly.

4. Tunisian Food Blogs

- **Taste of Tunisia:** A blog showcasing recipes and restaurant recommendations for local dishes.
- **Gourmet Tunisian:** Highlights trending restaurants, street food, and dining events.

Best For: Learning about traditional Tunisian cuisine and hidden gems from a local perspective.

5. Local Facebook Groups

- Groups like **"Tunis Foodies"** or **"Tunis Dining Club"** feature real-time recommendations and updates from locals and expats.
- Members often post about new restaurants, food festivals, and street food experiences.
  Best For: Engaging with a community of food enthusiasts and getting personal tips.

6. Google Maps

Website: www.google.com/maps
Overview:

- Displays restaurants near your location, along with reviews, photos, and operating hours.
- Provides directions and estimated travel time.
  Best For: Quick searches and locating eateries on the go.

7. Tunisian Tourism Board

Website: www.discovertunisia.com
Overview:

- Official website featuring cultural and culinary highlights of Tunis.
- Provides recommendations for restaurants that showcase traditional Tunisian flavors.
  Best For: Exploring curated suggestions for authentic local dining.

8. Yelp Tunisia

Website: www.yelp.com
Overview:

- Features restaurant reviews, photos, and user tips.
- Focuses on a variety of dining options, from street food to fine dining.

Best For: Reading candid reviews from diners.

9. Instagram

Hashtags to Follow:

- #TunisFoodie
- #TunisianCuisine
- #StreetFoodTunis

Overview:

- Discover trendy spots and popular dishes through Instagram's vibrant food community.
- Many restaurants have profiles showcasing their menus and ambiance.

Best For: Visual inspiration and staying updated on the latest dining trends.

10. Local Apps (Like Vynd)

Overview:

- Apps like Vynd are gaining popularity in Tunisia for restaurant recommendations, reviews, and delivery options.

Best For: Finding dining options tailored to specific tastes and dietary needs.

Overall, dining in Tunis is a vibrant journey through flavors, offering everything from traditional Tunisian delicacies to international cuisine, lively street food, and cozy cafés. The city's culinary scene reflects its rich cultural heritage and modern influences, ensuring options for all tastes and dietary preferences.

NIGHTLIFE AND ENTERTAINMENT IN TUNIS

Tunis offers a dynamic nightlife scene that combines modern entertainment with traditional Tunisian charm. From lively bars and chic lounges to cultural performances and serene night-time strolls, there's something for everyone to enjoy after dark. Here's a comprehensive guide to making the most of Tunis's nightlife.

Best Bars and Lounges in Tunis

Tunis is home to a growing number of bars and lounges that cater to a wide range of preferences. From lively venues with music and dancing to intimate spots with stunning views, the city has options to suit every mood. Here's a detailed guide to the best places to enjoy a drink, unwind, or experience Tunis's vibrant nightlife.

Le Carpe Diem

Located in the upscale neighborhood of La Marsa, Le Carpe Diem is a trendy hotspot perfect for both locals and visitors.

- **Ambiance**: The venue boasts a stylish interior and an outdoor garden space, offering a mix of relaxed and energetic vibes.
- **Entertainment**: With live DJs, themed nights, and occasional cultural events, it's a dynamic place to enjoy music and dancing.

- **Drinks and Food**: Their cocktail menu is creative, and they offer a selection of small plates that pair well with drinks.

The Cliff

Situated in La Goulette, The Cliff is a bar-lounge that offers breathtaking views of the Mediterranean.

- **Location**: Perched on a cliffside, it provides a serene atmosphere perfect for a romantic evening or a quiet drink with friends.
- **Specialty**: Known for its expertly crafted cocktails and a fine selection of wines and beers.
- **Why Visit**: The combination of the sea breeze, great drinks, and stunning sunsets makes this a must-visit spot.

The Blue Note

The Blue Note, located in downtown Tunis, is a haven for jazz and live music enthusiasts.

- **Ambiance**: This intimate venue has a cozy, vintage-inspired interior that adds to the charm.
- **Music**: Regular live performances feature jazz, blues, and occasionally Tunisian fusion music.
- **Drinks**: The bar serves classic cocktails, craft beers, and a curated wine list.

Yüka

Nestled in Gammarth, Yüka is a chic and modern lounge offering a mix of nightlife and fine dining.

- **Design**: The sleek décor and sophisticated lighting create an elegant ambiance.
- **Music and Events**: Yüka often hosts international DJs and themed parties, making it a lively spot for night owls.
- **Menu**: Their drink menu includes signature cocktails and an impressive range of spirits, paired with gourmet bites.

Boeuf sur le Toit

A long-standing favorite in Tunis, Boeuf sur le Toit combines dining, music, and a vibrant bar scene.

- **Ambiance**: With its warm lighting and plush seating, it's a great place for a relaxed yet upscale evening.
- **Live Entertainment**: The venue often features live jazz, pop, and local music acts.
- **Specialty**: Try their signature cocktails or explore the Tunisian wine offerings.

Villa Didon Bar

Located in the historical Carthage area, Villa Didon offers a luxurious setting with panoramic views of the ancient city and the sea.

- **Ambiance**: The bar's sleek and modern design, coupled with its scenic location, provides a refined experience.
- **Drinks**: Known for premium cocktails and an extensive wine list.
- **Why Visit**: Its upscale vibe makes it perfect for special occasions or a sophisticated night out.

Gatsby Bar

Situated in Gammarth, Gatsby Bar is a glamorous venue that exudes style and sophistication.

- **Theme**: The Great Gatsby-inspired décor creates a 1920s luxury feel.
- **Music and Events**: Expect live DJs, themed nights, and an energetic crowd.
- **Drinks**: The mixologists here are known for their innovative cocktails and unique flavor combinations.

Le Plug

A vibrant bar in downtown Tunis, Le Plug is a great place for casual nights and live music.

- **Ambiance**: A lively, youthful energy fills the space, with eclectic décor and a relaxed atmosphere.
- **Entertainment**: Live bands and DJs frequently perform, offering a mix of genres from rock to electronic music.
- **Drinks and Food**: Affordable cocktails and a selection of bar snacks make this spot popular among locals and tourists alike.

The Roof

Located atop a luxury hotel in the city center, The Roof offers a blend of panoramic views and chic nightlife.

- **Atmosphere**: The rooftop setting provides a perfect backdrop for sipping cocktails under the stars.
- **Specialty**: Known for their expertly crafted mojitos and martinis.

- **Why Visit**: The combination of stunning views, a vibrant atmosphere, and stylish décor makes it a standout venue.

Le Malouf

For a more traditional experience, Le Malouf is a bar that emphasizes Tunisian culture.

- **Ambiance**: Rustic and authentic, with traditional Tunisian music adding to the charm.
- **Menu**: Enjoy local wines, beers, and mezze platters.
- **Why Visit**: A great place to experience Tunisian hospitality and culture in a cozy setting.

Nightclubs and Live Music Venues in Tunis

Tunis has become an increasingly popular destination for those seeking exciting nightlife, especially for those who love music and dancing. From high-energy nightclubs to venues offering live music performances across various genres, the city offers an eclectic mix of entertainment options. Whether you're looking to dance until dawn or enjoy a more laid-back night with live tunes, here's a deeper look at the best nightclubs and live music venues in Tunis.

Calypso Club

Calypso Club in Gammarth is one of the most renowned nightclubs in Tunis, drawing both locals and tourists for its vibrant atmosphere.

- **Music**: The club offers a mix of international and local DJ performances, with electronic, house, and techno beats. They also host themed nights for a more diverse experience.
- **Dance Floor**: The massive dance floor gets packed, and the lighting and sound systems create an electrifying atmosphere.
- **Why Visit**: If you're looking for an all-night party, Calypso Club is the place to be. Expect world-class DJs, high-energy crowds, and a fun, upbeat ambiance.

Le Plug

Le Plug is a great venue for live music lovers who enjoy discovering new and upcoming bands or DJs.

- **Music**: The venue frequently hosts live performances, ranging from indie rock to pop, jazz, and alternative genres. DJs also perform, playing a variety of music, including electronic and contemporary hits.
- **Atmosphere**: The vibe is youthful and artistic, making it a favorite among locals who prefer a less mainstream experience. The casual setting encourages conversation, and the intimate stage setup makes it easy to interact with the performers.
- **Why Visit**: Le Plug is perfect for those looking for something different from the typical club scene. It's a venue where you can enjoy the music and discover the local music scene.

L'Agora

L'Agora is more than just a nightclub; it's a cultural venue where you can enjoy live music, theater, and film screenings.

- **Music**: The venue offers a mix of live music performances, with genres ranging from jazz to traditional Tunisian music and fusion. It's also a popular spot for artistic and experimental performances.
- **Cultural Events**: Beyond music, L'Agora regularly hosts events like poetry readings, local art exhibitions, and even dance performances, creating a vibrant cultural hub.
- **Why Visit**: If you appreciate live music performances in a laid-back yet creative environment, L'Agora offers an experience that mixes entertainment with cultural enrichment.

Pacha Tunis

Pacha Tunis, part of the world-famous Pacha nightclub chain, offers a truly international nightclub experience.

- **Music**: Known for its diverse electronic music, Pacha hosts world-class DJs spinning house, techno, and trance beats. The club is famed for its laser shows and immersive sound system, creating an unforgettable dance experience.
- **Venue**: With multiple dance floors and private VIP areas, Pacha offers something for everyone, whether you're into dancing or simply relaxing in an exclusive lounge.
- **Why Visit**: If you're a fan of large-scale nightclubs with top-tier DJs, Pacha is the perfect place for you. The club attracts an international crowd, offering a lively, cosmopolitan vibe.

Le Bardo Club

Le Bardo Club is an elegant nightclub known for its refined ambiance and upscale clientele.

- **Music**: Le Bardo features a mix of live jazz, deep house, and international hits, making it a favorite for those who enjoy sophisticated nightlife with a focus on music.
- **Exclusive Environment**: With its plush seating, VIP sections, and elegant décor, Le Bardo appeals to those seeking a high-end, intimate clubbing experience.
- **Why Visit**: If you're looking for a chic night out with great music in an exclusive environment, Le Bardo Club is one of the best options in Tunis.

The Blue Note

For lovers of jazz and live music, The Blue Note is a hidden gem in the heart of Tunis.

- **Music**: The venue features live jazz performances and occasionally hosts other genres such as blues and soul. The relaxed, intimate atmosphere makes it an ideal spot for music aficionados.
- **Ambiance**: With its soft lighting and small, intimate setting, The Blue Note offers a cozy atmosphere perfect for enjoying a drink while listening to smooth jazz.
- **Why Visit**: If you're a fan of live music in a chill, intimate environment, The Blue Note is an essential stop. It's perfect for those seeking a quieter, more cultural nightlife experience.

Cultural Evening Experiences in Tunis

Tunis is a city rich in history and culture, offering visitors a variety of unique cultural evening experiences. Whether you are interested in traditional Tunisian music, local cuisine, or exploring the city's historical sites under the moonlight, there are plenty of options to dive deeper into Tunis's cultural fabric after dark. Below are some of the most enriching and memorable cultural evening experiences you can enjoy in Tunis.

Traditional Tunisian Music Performances

Tunisia has a long and rich tradition of music, with the **Muwashshah** (traditional Andalusian music), **Malouf** (classical Tunisian music), and **Raï** being some of the most beloved genres.

- **Where to Experience**:
    - **Café de la Musique**: Located in the medina of Tunis, this venue hosts live performances of traditional Tunisian music.
    - **The National Theatre of Tunisia**: Frequently puts on cultural performances, including traditional music concerts, during the evening.
- **Why Visit**: These performances provide an intimate way to experience the cultural heritage of Tunisia. The music is an essential aspect of the country's identity, and listening to it live in a traditional setting allows visitors to connect more deeply with the culture.

Evening at the Bardo Museum

The Bardo Museum, known for its extensive collection of Roman mosaics, is one of the most famous museums in Tunisia. It offers visitors a chance to explore Tunis's rich archaeological history in the evening during special events.

- **Special Events**:
    - **Evening Museum Tours**: The museum occasionally offers evening tours for a more peaceful experience, with fewer crowds.
    - **Cultural Nights**: The Bardo often hosts special cultural nights with live performances, talks, and music inspired by ancient traditions.
- **Why Visit**: The Bardo Museum in the evening offers a serene atmosphere to appreciate the artworks and historical exhibits. The occasional cultural performances enhance the experience, giving you a unique insight into Tunisia's past.

Tunisian Dinner with Folk Music

For an immersive cultural experience, enjoy a traditional Tunisian dinner while being entertained by live folk music and dance. Many restaurants and cultural centers around Tunis host themed dinner nights, where you can enjoy local dishes while watching performances of Tunisian folk dances like the **Raqs al-Sha'bi**.

- **Where to Experience**:
    - **Dar El Jeld**: A well-known restaurant in the heart of the Medina, offering traditional Tunisian dishes paired with live performances of classical Tunisian music and belly dancing.
    - **Restaurant El Menzah**: Known for its authentic Tunisian cuisine and live traditional music.
- **Why Visit**: These cultural dinner experiences allow visitors to taste local dishes such as couscous, brik, and harissa

while experiencing the vibrant folk music and dance traditions that are an integral part of Tunisian culture.

Sunset at the Ruins of Carthage

The ancient ruins of Carthage, a UNESCO World Heritage site, offer a magical experience in the evening, especially at sunset. The historical significance and beauty of the site come to life as the sun dips below the horizon, casting a golden hue over the ruins.

- **Special Events**:
  - **Evening Tours**: Some tour operators offer sunset tours to the ruins, which are perfect for those interested in history, culture, and photography.
  - **Cultural Performances**: Occasionally, the ruins host open-air concerts or performances inspired by Carthaginian history and mythology.
- **Why Visit**: Watching the sunset at the ruins of Carthage is a moment of serenity, offering a beautiful blend of natural beauty and ancient history. The evening light adds a romantic and reflective quality to the site.

Traditional Tunisian Theatre and Performing Arts

Tunis has a vibrant theater scene that reflects both the modern and traditional aspects of Tunisian culture. The **Tunis Opera House** and **Municipal Theatre of Tunis** are two prime locations to experience local and international performances.

- **What to Expect**:
  - **Traditional Tunisian Plays**: Often focusing on local customs, folklore, and societal themes.

- o **Modern and Experimental Performances**: Many venues also offer contemporary works, showcasing the country's evolving cultural scene.
- o **Ballet and Dance**: The Opera House frequently hosts ballet and contemporary dance performances, often incorporating traditional Tunisian movements with modern choreography.
- **Why Visit**: For those interested in the arts, a night at the theater offers a sophisticated way to experience Tunisia's cultural depth through storytelling, music, and dance.

Sufi Music and Dance

Sufism, a form of Islamic mysticism, has deep roots in Tunisia. One of the most fascinating cultural experiences in Tunis is witnessing a **Sufi music and dance** performance, most famously the **Whirling Dervishes**, which is both a spiritual and artistic expression.

- **Where to Experience**:
  - o **Sidi Mahrez Mosque**: Hosts occasional Sufi music and dance performances, particularly during religious festivals.
  - o **Dar Ben Gacem**: A cultural center in the medina that offers performances of traditional Sufi music and spiritual dance.
- **Why Visit**: Sufi performances are mesmerizing and spiritually uplifting. The combination of music, rhythm, and dance provides an insight into the mystical side of Tunisian culture, making it an unforgettable experience.

Night Walks Through the Medina

The **Medina of Tunis**, a UNESCO World Heritage site, offers a magical experience in the evening, as the winding alleyways and traditional buildings take on a mystical feel under the streetlights.

- **Special Events**:
    - **Night Walks and Cultural Tours**: Some local tour guides offer evening walks through the Medina, where you can learn about the history, architecture, and local crafts while exploring the quieter side of the old city.
    - **Crafts and Souks**: As night falls, some of the souks (markets) come alive with night vendors selling handmade goods, jewelry, and fabrics.
- **Why Visit**: Walking through the Medina in the evening gives you a sense of the city's history and culture, while the cooler night air and quieter atmosphere make it a serene way to explore.

Tunis's nightlife offers a perfect blend of culture, relaxation, and excitement. Whether you're seeking an energetic party scene, a cultural performance, or a quiet night with stunning views, the city caters to all preferences. With proper planning and an open mind, your evenings in Tunis can become unforgettable highlights of your trip.

SHOPPING IN TUNIS

Tunis is a vibrant city that offers an eclectic mix of shopping experiences, from bustling traditional markets to modern shopping malls. It doesn't matter if you're looking for unique souvenirs, local handicrafts, or high-end international brands, Tunis has something for everyone. Here's a comprehensive guide to shopping in Tunis, with essential tips and information for tourists.

Traditional Souks and Markets in Tunis

Tunis' traditional souks and markets are vibrant hubs of commerce and culture, offering visitors an authentic glimpse into the country's rich history and craftsmanship. These markets, located primarily within the historic Medina of Tunis, are a maze of narrow alleyways filled with centuries-old shops selling everything from handmade textiles to intricate jewelry, spices, and local produce. Here's a deeper dive into the souks and markets of Tunis, providing essential tips for navigating these bustling shopping districts.

The Medina

The Medina of Tunis is a UNESCO World Heritage site and home to some of the city's most famous and historical souks. Dating back to the 7th century, the Medina retains its traditional layout, with narrow streets and alleyways that are packed with small shops and workshops. Here, you can find a wide range of goods, from everyday items to luxury handcrafted goods. It's an area where the old and the new coexist, with modern conveniences existing alongside centuries-old traditions.

- **Architecture of the Medina:** The souks are housed in beautiful buildings with traditional Tunisian architecture—arches, intricate tilework, and beautiful doors—that reflect the history and culture of the city. As you explore, take time to admire the architecture while shopping.
- **Navigating the Medina:** The maze-like structure of the Medina can be overwhelming, so it's recommended to take your time. If you're visiting for the first time, consider hiring a local guide to help you navigate the narrow streets and alleyways. Many guides can also provide insights into the history behind the different souks and products.

Notable Souks in the Medina

Here are some of the key souks in Tunis, each offering unique products that reflect the rich cultural and artisan traditions of Tunisia:

- **Souk El Attarine:** One of the most famous souks in the Medina, Souk El Attarine specializes in traditional perfumes and essential oils, many of which are made from local flowers and herbs. This is the place to purchase high-quality, locally-made scents, including rose water, jasmine, and amber. The souk also sells spices, herbs, and incense, making it a sensory experience for shoppers.
- **Souk des Tailleurs:** Known for its leather goods, Souk des Tailleurs is a must-visit for those looking to purchase finely crafted leather jackets, bags, shoes, belts, and wallets. These items are made by local artisans using traditional

techniques passed down through generations. The leather products in this souk are renowned for their high quality, durability, and unique designs.

- **Souk El Berka:** This souk is known for its traditional Tunisian antiques, such as old coins, handcrafted jewelry, and vintage items. Here, visitors can find unique treasures, including old silverware, lamps, and carpets. Souk El Berka is also an excellent place to find beautiful handmade textiles, including scarves, shawls, and embroidered linens.
- **Souk des Chéchias:** The chechia, a traditional red felt hat worn by Tunisians, is a staple of local culture. Souk des Chéchias is where you'll find this iconic hat, crafted from wool and felt. The hats are often sold in vibrant colors, including red, white, and black, and are available in different sizes. This souk offers a perfect souvenir for those wanting to take home a piece of Tunisian heritage.
- **Souk El Fekka:** A hidden gem in the Medina, Souk El Fekka specializes in fine Tunisian fabrics, particularly silks and cottons. This souk offers a range of textiles used for making traditional clothing like the **jebba** (a type of tunic), **sarouel** (baggy trousers), and **fouta** (a traditional Tunisian towel). You can also find a variety of beautiful scarves and bed linens.
- **Souk Al Ghoula:** A smaller souk, Al Ghoula is known for its collection of Tunisian jewelry, particularly silver. The souk features a variety of traditional Berber designs, with intricate engravings and gemstone settings. Silver jewelry is an essential part of Tunisian culture, and this souk offers some of the most exquisite examples.

The Souk Experience

Shopping in Tunisian souks is a unique experience that goes beyond just purchasing goods—it's a sensory journey through color, sound, and scent. Here are some key aspects of shopping in these traditional markets:

- **Vibrant Atmosphere:** The souks are typically busy, filled with locals bargaining, shopkeepers calling out to potential customers, and the scent of spices, perfumes, and fresh produce wafting through the air. It's an immersive experience that captures the essence of Tunisian life.
- **Friendly and Engaging Vendors:** Shopkeepers in the souks are often friendly and eager to engage with customers, offering a warm welcome to visitors. Many vendors will greet you with a smile and invite you into their shops with a display of their best wares. It's a good idea to engage in friendly conversation—locals are often proud to share stories about their craft and the history of their goods.
- **Bargaining Culture:** Bargaining is an integral part of the shopping experience in the souks. Vendors expect visitors to negotiate prices, so don't be afraid to haggle. Start by offering a price that's half of what the vendor is asking and work your way up. Keep the tone friendly and respectful, and remember that it's all part of the fun of shopping in the souks.
- **Time of Visit:** The souks can get crowded, especially during peak tourist season. For a more relaxed shopping experience, try visiting early in the morning or later in the afternoon, when the crowds are thinner, and the temperatures are cooler. Also, many souks are quieter in the early evening, making it an excellent time for a leisurely stroll through the market.

Tips for Shopping in Tunisian Souks

To make the most of your shopping experience in Tunisian souks, here are some practical tips to keep in mind:

- **Know What You're Looking For:** While the souks are a great place to explore, it's also easy to get distracted by the wide variety of goods on offer. If you have a particular item in mind, such as a specific type of pottery or textile, make sure you keep focused to avoid feeling overwhelmed.
- **Cash is King:** While some larger shops may accept credit cards, most souks operate on a cash-only basis, and it's best to carry Tunisian dinars (TND). ATMs are available around the city, but it's always advisable to carry enough cash with you when you head to the souks.
- **Wear Comfortable Shoes:** The Medina's streets are often uneven, with cobblestones and narrow passages, so it's important to wear comfortable shoes while shopping. Be prepared to walk a lot as you explore the various souks.
- **Stay Hydrated:** Shopping in the souks can be physically demanding, especially during the hot summer months. Be sure to carry a bottle of water and take breaks to avoid exhaustion.
- **Be Respectful of Local Culture:** Tunisian souks are deeply tied to local traditions and culture, so it's important to be respectful of customs. Photography may be restricted in some shops, especially when it comes to the artisans working with delicate materials like textiles or pottery, so always ask before snapping a photo.

Modern Shopping Malls and Retail Centers

While Tunis is widely known for its traditional souks and vibrant markets, it also offers a range of modern shopping malls and retail centers that cater to those seeking contemporary shopping experiences. These malls blend international brands with local offerings, making them an ideal choice for those looking for convenience, variety, and the latest fashion trends. Below is an expanded guide to some of the best modern shopping malls and retail centers in Tunis, providing you with essential tips and information to navigate the city's contemporary shopping scene.

La Marsa Shopping Mall

Located in the upscale district of La Marsa, just north of central Tunis, **La Marsa Shopping Mall** is one of the city's most modern retail destinations. The mall offers a mix of international brands, local boutiques, and dining options, making it a one-stop shopping spot for locals and tourists alike.

- **What to Expect:**
    - **Retail Stores:** La Marsa Shopping Mall hosts well-known international brands, such as **H&M**, **Zara**, **C&A**, and **Max & Co.**, offering everything from stylish clothing to footwear and accessories. You'll also find local Tunisian fashion brands, providing a mix of contemporary and traditional designs.
    - **Electronics and Gadgets:** For tech enthusiasts, the mall has several stores dedicated to electronics, offering the latest smartphones, computers, and gadgets at competitive prices.

- ○ **Dining Options:** After a shopping spree, visitors can relax and enjoy a meal at one of the mall's cafes or restaurants, many of which offer a range of local and international cuisines. Whether you're in the mood for traditional Tunisian food or a quick bite from a global fast-food chain, there's something for everyone.
- ○ **Family-Friendly Activities:** La Marsa Shopping Mall also has a dedicated children's play area and an entertainment section with movie theaters, making it a great spot for families.
- **Tips for Shopping at La Marsa Mall:**
  - ○ **Sales and Discounts:** The best time to shop for deals is during the seasonal sales, typically in January and July, when stores offer significant discounts on clothing, electronics, and accessories.
  - ○ **Accessibility:** La Marsa is well-connected to central Tunis by public transport, but if you prefer a more direct route, taxis are readily available. If you're staying in the La Marsa area, it's easy to walk to the mall.

Carrefour Tunis

Carrefour Tunis is a large, modern shopping complex located in the center of the city. It combines a hypermarket with a variety of retail outlets, making it a perfect destination for a mix of practical shopping and leisurely browsing. Carrefour is a popular destination for both locals and tourists seeking a broad selection of goods at affordable prices.

- **What to Expect:**
  - **Hypermarket:** The Carrefour hypermarket offers a wide range of groceries, household goods, clothing, and electronics. It's an ideal place to stock up on essentials, including fresh produce, packaged food, cleaning supplies, and personal care products.
  - **Retail Stores:** In addition to the hypermarket, Carrefour Tunis is home to numerous stores selling clothing, shoes, cosmetics, and home goods. International fashion brands like **Tiffany & Co.**, **Adidas**, and **Lacoste** have their own dedicated spaces here, offering a wide range of clothing and accessories for men, women, and children.
  - **Electronics and Gadgets:** Carrefour also houses stores specializing in electronics, from the latest smartphones and laptops to televisions and home appliances. It's a good spot for tech shoppers looking for gadgets or appliances at competitive prices.
- **Tips for Shopping at Carrefour Tunis:**
  - **One-Stop Shopping:** If you're looking to buy both practical items (such as groceries and household products) and fashion or electronics, Carrefour Tunis is a great one-stop shop.
  - **Quality of Products:** While Carrefour offers a mix of local and international products, make sure to compare prices for similar items across different stores in the mall, especially if you're looking for premium products or specific brands.

City of Culture Mall (Cité de la Culture)

The **City of Culture Mall** is part of the larger **Cité de la Culture**, a major cultural and artistic hub in Tunis. Located near the historic center of the city, this mall offers a unique blend of contemporary shopping and cultural experiences. It's an excellent choice for those looking to explore Tunisian art and culture alongside modern retail outlets.

- **What to Expect:**
  - **Art and Craft Shops:** Located in the cultural center, many shops in the City of Culture Mall sell works of Tunisian artists, including paintings, sculptures, and handcrafted goods. Visitors will find a variety of local art, crafts, and souvenirs that reflect Tunisia's cultural heritage.
  - **Fashion and Jewelry:** The mall also features several clothing boutiques, selling trendy local and international fashion brands. Jewelry stores specializing in gold and silver pieces, often influenced by Tunisian design, are also prominent in the mall.
  - **Cultural Events and Performances:** In addition to shopping, the City of Culture Mall regularly hosts cultural events, performances, and exhibitions. Visitors can enjoy a blend of shopping and entertainment, making it a great place to spend an afternoon.
- **Tips for Shopping at City of Culture Mall:**
  - **Explore Local Art:** Take time to explore the local art galleries and craft shops within the mall. You can find one-of-a-kind pieces of Tunisian art and craftwork, including jewelry, paintings, and textiles.
  - **Check the Calendar:** If you're interested in attending cultural events or performances, check the City of Culture's calendar to see what's happening during your

visit. These events often coincide with shopping, providing a well-rounded experience.

Tunis City Mall

Located in the heart of Tunis, **Tunis City Mall** is a modern shopping center that offers a mix of high-end brands, a variety of dining options, and entertainment facilities. The mall is popular among both locals and tourists, especially those seeking luxury shopping experiences.

- **What to Expect:**
    - **Luxury and International Brands:** Tunis City Mall is home to several luxury fashion brands, including **Chanel**, **Louis Vuitton**, **Gucci**, and **Burberry**. These high-end stores are complemented by boutiques offering premium watches, jewelry, and accessories.
    - **Dining Options:** The mall has a number of restaurants and cafes serving both Tunisian and international cuisine. After a shopping spree, you can enjoy a coffee or meal at one of the stylish eateries within the mall.
    - **Entertainment Facilities:** The mall features a cinema, making it a great place to unwind after a day of shopping. It also houses arcades and play zones for children, adding to its family-friendly atmosphere.
- **Tips for Shopping at Tunis City Mall:**
    - **Luxury Goods:** If you're looking to splurge on high-end items, Tunis City Mall offers the best selection of luxury goods in the city. Be sure to check for seasonal sales or exclusive deals at your favorite brands.
    - **Explore the Dining Scene:** Don't miss the opportunity to explore the mall's diverse dining options. From fine

dining to casual cafes, the food scene at Tunis City Mall is as diverse as its retail offerings.

Mall of Tunisia (Le Mall de Tunisie)

Located in the suburb of Ariana, just outside Tunis, Le Mall de Tunisie is one of the largest and most modern shopping malls in the country. This expansive retail center offers a blend of shopping, entertainment, and leisure activities, making it one of the most popular destinations for both locals and tourists.

- **What to Expect:**
    - **Wide Range of Stores:** Le Mall de Tunisie houses a mix of international retail chains, including **H&M**, **Gap**, **Nike**, **Sephora**, and **Fnac**, offering clothing, electronics, cosmetics, and home goods.
    - **Entertainment:** The mall features a multi-screen cinema, bowling alley, and indoor amusement park, making it a great place for family outings. There are also regular events and exhibitions held throughout the year.
    - **Dining:** With a diverse range of restaurants and food courts, Le Mall de Tunisie offers a selection of Tunisian and international food. It's a great place to enjoy everything from local delicacies to international fast food.
- **Tips for Shopping at Le Mall de Tunisie:**
    - **Weekend Crowds:** This mall can get crowded on weekends, especially during the evening. To avoid the hustle and bustle, plan your shopping trip for weekday mornings or afternoons.

- Entertainment Options: If you're traveling with children or looking for a fun family day out, take advantage of the mall's entertainment facilities. The cinema and amusement park are especially popular with families.

Tunisian Souvenirs to Take Home

When visiting Tunis, one of the best ways to remember your trip is by bringing home a piece of Tunisian culture through locally made souvenirs. From handcrafted jewelry to artisanal goods, there's no shortage of unique items to choose from. Whether you're shopping at traditional souks or modern retail centers, here's an expanded guide to the most popular Tunisian souvenirs and tips for making your selections.

Traditional Tunisian Pottery

Tunisian pottery, known for its vibrant colors and intricate designs, makes for a stunning and meaningful souvenir. The pottery in Tunisia varies by region, but the most famous pieces come from places like **Nabeul** and **Nefta**, where artisans use centuries-old techniques passed down through generations.

- **What to Look For:**
    - **Hand-painted Ceramics:** Look for plates, bowls, and decorative tiles with bold, geometric patterns or floral motifs. The use of bright blues, reds, and greens, often combined with intricate detailing, makes these pieces stand out.
    - **Tagine Pots:** A traditional cooking vessel used in Tunisia for slow-cooking stews, these clay pots are

often beautifully decorated and make both functional and decorative souvenirs.
- **Vases and Jugs:** Large decorative vases or jugs, often painted with scenes of Tunisian life or landscapes, are also highly sought after.

- **Tip:** When buying pottery, be sure to check for cracks or damage, as some handmade pieces can be fragile. Look for pieces that have a glossy, smooth finish, as this indicates a higher-quality glaze.

Tunisian Carpets and Rugs

Tunisian carpets are famous for their quality and craftsmanship, often woven by hand using wool or silk. The designs vary by region, with **Kairouan** being particularly famous for its fine carpets. These textiles are deeply rooted in the country's cultural heritage and represent a blend of Berber, Arab, and Mediterranean influences.

- **What to Look For:**
  - **Berber Rugs:** Featuring geometric patterns and muted colors, Berber rugs are traditionally handmade and are prized for their durability. These rugs often have deep cultural significance, with each design telling a story or symbolizing specific traditions.
  - **Kairouan Carpets:** Known for their high quality and intricate designs, these carpets are often woven with geometric and floral motifs. They come in a variety of sizes and colors, with some carpets incorporating gold and silver threads for added luxury.

- - Silk Rugs: These rugs are softer and more delicate than wool ones and can be found in shops in Tunis. They often feature intricate, detailed patterns, making them perfect for collectors or as a luxurious gift.
- Tip: Carpets and rugs can be large and cumbersome to transport, so consider the size and shipping options before making a purchase. Many stores offer international shipping, which can save you the hassle of carrying them home.

Tunisian Jewelry and Silverware

Tunisian jewelry is a popular souvenir due to its rich designs and cultural significance. Silver jewelry is especially common and is often crafted with intricate patterns or inlaid with semi-precious stones like turquoise or coral. Many pieces are inspired by ancient Carthaginian designs or Berber traditions, making them a perfect way to bring a piece of Tunisia's history home with you.

- **What to Look For:**
  - **Silver Jewelry:** Bracelets, necklaces, rings, and earrings featuring geometric designs, filigree work, or beads made from stones like **coral**, **turquoise**, or **amber** are typical of Tunisian jewelry. These pieces often carry symbolic meanings, such as protection or good fortune.
  - **Amulet Necklaces:** A traditional Tunisian amulet, called the **khamsa** or **Hand of Fatima**, is a popular souvenir. This symbol is believed to ward off the evil eye and bring good luck.

- o **Tunisian Berber Rings and Pendants:** Large, statement rings and pendants, often incorporating colorful stones and detailed metalwork, are highly collectible and unique to Tunisia.
- **Tip:** Be cautious when purchasing jewelry to ensure that the silver is genuine. Ask for certification if you're unsure of the authenticity, especially if buying higher-end items.

Handwoven Fabrics and Textiles

Tunisia has a rich tradition of textile production, and you can find a variety of handwoven fabrics and garments in local markets. From **cotton** and **linen** to **wool** and **silk**, the quality of Tunisian textiles is exceptional.

- **What to Look For:**
  - o **Fouta Towels:** These versatile handwoven towels are made from cotton or linen and are often brightly striped in bold colors. They are perfect for the beach, but they can also be used as scarves, tablecloths, or even as a decorative throw.
  - o **Tunisia's Traditional Embroidered Fabrics:** Many garments, especially women's dresses and headscarves, are embellished with delicate embroidery in bright colors. These items often reflect the cultural heritage of different regions, such as the coastal cities of **Sousse** or **Monastir**.
  - o **Sufra:** A traditional, handwoven textile, often used for tablecloths or home decor, Sufra textiles are

made with cotton and wool, and they come in vibrant colors with geometric patterns.
- **Tip:** If you're looking for textiles, visit **Sidi Bou Said**, a coastal town near Tunis, known for its handwoven products. Be sure to inspect the fabric quality to ensure you're purchasing authentic, handmade items.

Olive Oil and Tunisian Spices

Tunisian olive oil is world-renowned for its quality, making it an excellent souvenir to bring back home. The country's Mediterranean climate and fertile soil contribute to the production of premium olive oil, often recognized for its fruity, rich taste.

- **What to Look For:**
    - **Olive Oil:** Look for **extra virgin olive oil** from local farms. It is often sold in decorative bottles, making it easy to bring home. Many stores also offer olive oil-based beauty products, such as soaps and lotions.
    - **Spices:** Tunisia's vibrant cuisine is characterized by rich, aromatic spices. **Harissa**, a spicy chili paste, is a must-buy for those who want to recreate Tunisian dishes at home. You can also find **cumin**, **saffron**, and **coriander** in most spice shops.
- **Tip:** If you're buying olive oil, make sure to select a bottle that's well sealed and packaged to avoid leaks during travel. Spices like harissa are easy to carry and make great gifts for food enthusiasts.

Traditional Tunisian Clothing

Tunisian clothing is deeply influenced by the country's history and its blend of Arab, Berber, and Mediterranean cultures. From traditional garments to modern interpretations, these clothes are not only stylish but also steeped in tradition.

- **What to Look For:**
    - **Fouta and Blouza:** These are traditional garments worn by both men and women. The **fouta** is a wraparound skirt or sarong, and the **blouza** is a type of loose blouse or tunic. They are often made of lightweight cotton or linen and come in a variety of colors and patterns.
    - **Jebba:** A traditional, embroidered robe often worn by men, the **jebba** is a long, flowing garment with a hood, typically worn on special occasions. It can be found in both simple and intricate designs.
    - **Kaftans:** Elegant and flowing, the **kaftan** is a traditional garment worn by women, often embroidered with gold thread. It is a beautiful garment for both formal and casual settings.
- **Tip:** When purchasing traditional clothing, ensure that the fabric feels comfortable and breathable, especially if you plan to wear it in warm climates. Custom tailoring options are available in many markets for a personalized fit.

Tunisian Sweet Treats and Confectioneries

Tunisian sweets are an indulgent treat for those with a sweet tooth. From pastries to rich confections, they make delightful souvenirs to bring back or to enjoy on the go.

- **What to Look For:**

- - Makroud: A popular sweet made from semolina, dates, and almonds, often deep-fried and coated with honey or sugar syrup. It's a must-try dessert that you can easily carry home.
  - Baklava: Layers of flaky pastry, honey, and nuts make Tunisian baklava a delicious gift for those who enjoy rich desserts.
  - Dates and Figs: Tunisia is famous for its high-quality dates, especially the **deglet nour** variety. Figs, dried and coated with sugar, also make a tasty treat to bring home.
- Tip: When purchasing sweets or dried fruit, look for sealed packaging to maintain freshness. These items are a great way to share a taste of Tunisia with friends and family back home.

Shopping for Luxury Goods in Tunis

Tunis offers a refined shopping experience for those seeking luxury goods, combining the opulence of high-end international brands with the elegance of local craftsmanship. Whether you're searching for exclusive designer fashion, fine jewelry, luxury watches, or upscale home décor, Tunis provides a range of shopping options that cater to discerning tastes. The city's luxury shopping scene reflects a blend of modern sophistication and traditional Tunisian flair, offering shoppers an opportunity to indulge in luxury while also embracing local culture.

High-End Fashion and Designer Boutiques

Tunis is home to several high-end fashion boutiques, offering a curated selection of international designer brands as well as a few exclusive local fashion labels. These boutiques are typically located in the city's upscale districts, such as **Ariana** and the **Lake of Tunis** area, where discerning shoppers can find a variety of luxury clothing, footwear, and accessories.

- **What to Look For:**
  - **International Designer Brands:** In the upscale shopping centers and boutiques, you'll find a range of global fashion labels like **Chanel**, **Louis Vuitton**, **Gucci**, and **Prada**. These brands are renowned for their impeccable quality and timeless style.
  - **Local Luxury Fashion Designers:** Tunisia also has a growing fashion scene, with talented local designers producing exclusive collections that reflect Tunisian culture and craftsmanship. Look for pieces made with traditional fabrics like **safsari** (a woven fabric) or **silk**.
  - **Tailored Garments:** Many high-end shops offer personalized tailoring services, where you can have garments adjusted to your measurements for a perfect fit.
- **Tip:** When shopping for luxury fashion items, check if the boutique offers after-sales services, such as repairs or care instructions, for the upkeep of high-end garments and accessories.

Fine Jewelry and Watches

Tunis is home to a variety of jewelry stores that feature both local and international luxury jewelry collections. Whether you're looking for exquisite handcrafted pieces using traditional Tunisian designs or international brands renowned for their luxury, you'll find a wide selection in the city's high-end shopping districts.

- **What to Look For:**
    - **Traditional Tunisian Jewelry:** Tunisian jewelry often features bold, intricate designs with symbolic motifs. Silver and gold pieces such as cufflinks, necklaces, and earrings are commonly adorned with turquoise or amber stones, representing local craftsmanship and Tunisian artistry.
    - **Luxury International Brands:** For those interested in high-end international luxury, stores in Tunis carry famous brands such as Cartier, Rolex, and Patek Philippe. These jewelry and watch pieces are crafted from the finest materials and represent timeless luxury.
    - **Custom Jewelry:** Many local jewelers offer the opportunity to design bespoke pieces, creating one-of-a-kind jewelry that incorporates Tunisian artistry alongside modern aesthetics.
- **Tip:** When purchasing fine jewelry or watches, always inquire about the authenticity and certification of precious stones and metals. If you're buying a luxury watch, ensure that it comes with the brand's warranty and paperwork.

Luxury Leather Goods and Accessories

Leather goods are an important part of Tunisian craftsmanship, with high-quality, handmade leather products available at select boutiques. From elegant bags and briefcases to wallets and belts, Tunis offers an array of luxury leather items that combine style with function.

- **What to Look For:**
  - **Handmade Leather Bags:** Opt for exclusive leather handbags and totes crafted by local artisans, often featuring intricate stitching and unique designs. Many leather products are made from genuine Tunisian leather and feature detailed embellishments such as gold or silver hardware.
  - **Leather Shoes and Boots:** Luxury leather footwear, including custom-made shoes, suits, and boots, are available at boutique stores in Tunis. These items are known for their durability and impeccable craftsmanship.
  - **Accessories:** Luxury leather goods also include wallets, belts, and keychains. Many of these are produced with an attention to detail and can make for stylish and timeless gifts or souvenirs.
- **Tip:** Leather products tend to be long-lasting, so ensure you're purchasing items made with the finest quality leather. Check the lining and stitching to confirm the craftsmanship.

Luxury Home Décor and Art

For those looking to adorn their homes with high-end furniture and accessories, Tunis offers a variety of luxury home décor shops. These stores feature imported designer furniture, art pieces, and decorative items, as well as locally crafted luxury goods that reflect Tunisia's cultural heritage.

- **What to Look For:**
  - **Imported Furniture:** High-end furniture stores in Tunis carry collections from renowned designers

and international brands. Expect to find sophisticated pieces, such as luxury sofas, wooden coffee tables, and chandeliers that blend modern design with classic elegance.
- **Traditional Tunisian Art:** Tunisian artists often blend contemporary and traditional techniques, producing stunning artwork that can serve as a focal point in any room. Look for hand-painted ceramics, wooden carvings, and woven textiles that offer a unique, artistic touch.
- **Luxury Home Accessories:** Think vintage glassware, fine china, and handcrafted rugs. These items are crafted with attention to detail and are designed to add a luxurious flair to any living space.
- **Tip:** When purchasing high-end home décor, especially artwork or furniture, check the authenticity and provenance of the item. Inquire if the piece is a limited edition or comes with a certificate of authenticity.

Designer Perfumes and Fragrances

Tunis boasts a variety of perfume boutiques where luxury fragrances are sold, catering to those who appreciate the art of scent. Many of these stores carry **international perfume houses** as well as **local Tunisian perfumers** who create unique, bespoke fragrances that blend regional influences with modern elegance.

- **What to Look For:**
  - **International Perfume Brands:** Luxury perfume brands such as Chanel, Dior, and Tom Ford are available in upscale department stores and perfume shops throughout the city. These brands offer

classic and contemporary scents for both men and women.
- **Tunisian-Produced Fragrances:** Tunisia is known for producing high-quality perfumes using local ingredients like jasmine, rose, and orange blossom. Many of these perfumes are crafted by local artisans and offer a distinctly Tunisian scent experience.
- **Custom Fragrance Blends:** Some high-end perfume boutiques offer personalized fragrance services, where you can create a custom scent tailored to your tastes and preferences.
- **Tip:** When shopping for luxury perfumes, always test the fragrance before purchasing and ask for sample sizes if available. Perfumes tend to evolve over time, so ensure the scent is something you'll enjoy wearing long-term.

Luxury Shopping Malls and Retail Centers

Tunis has a growing number of luxury shopping malls and retail centers, where international and local luxury brands are available under one roof. These shopping centers offer a modern, high-end experience, complete with upscale dining options, spas, and entertainment.

- **What to Look For:**
  - **Carrefour Tunis City:** A high-end mall that features both international luxury brands and exclusive local boutiques. The mall is an excellent place for shopping, dining, and enjoying other amenities such as cinemas and spas.
  - **Le Passage Mall:** Located in downtown Tunis, this upscale mall offers designer fashion, luxury

- jewelry, and exclusive beauty products. It is popular for its spacious layout and high-quality retail stores.
  - **Carthage Mall:** Known for its luxury fashion and beauty boutiques, Carthage Mall is a stylish shopping destination where visitors can find top-tier international brands alongside high-end Tunisian retailers.
- **Tip:** When shopping in luxury malls, take advantage of concierge services, which can help you find specific items, provide personal styling advice, or even arrange for private shopping experiences.

Shopping in Tunis offers a delightful blend of traditional and modern experiences, ensuring that there's something for every traveler. Whether you're wandering through the Medina's lively souks or browsing sleek shopping malls, make sure to bargain in the souks, check the authenticity of artisan goods, and enjoy the rich variety of Tunisian culture reflected in its products.

CULTURAL EXPERIENCES IN TUNIS

Tunis offers an enriching blend of history, tradition, and modern-day culture. For travelers eager to experience the heart of Tunisia, immersing themselves in the local culture is a must. Here are some key cultural experiences in Tunis that every visitor should explore.

Traditional Hammams

Tunis, like much of the Mediterranean and the Arab world, has a rich history of using hammams (traditional steam baths) as both a form of relaxation and a key social activity. The hammam is a cultural institution that has been a central part of daily life for centuries, providing a communal space for cleansing, unwinding, and socializing. While modern spas have emerged in the city, the traditional hammam experience still holds an important place in Tunisian culture.

The History and Significance of Hammams

Hammams trace their roots to ancient Roman bathhouses, with the concept refined by the Ottomans and Arabs, who perfected the art of communal bathing as part of daily life. Historically, hammams were not just places for bathing but also important social spaces where men and women gathered to talk, relax, and maintain personal hygiene. In Tunis, hammams remain integral to local life, particularly for residents in the Medina (the historic old city), where many traditional bathhouses still operate today.

- **Cultural Importance:**
    - Hammams were seen as places for cleansing not only the body but also the soul, with many people visiting for weekly or monthly baths.
    - In Tunisia, the hammam experience is also a significant social ritual. People often visit with family or friends, enjoying conversations and relaxation together.
    - Traditionally, the hammam has also been a space for special occasions such as weddings, where women prepare for the event by attending a hammam for beauty rituals.

The Hammam Experience: What to Expect

A visit to a traditional hammam in Tunis is much more than a simple bath. It is a multi-sensory experience that focuses on cleansing and rejuvenating both the body and mind. Below is a step-by-step guide to what you can expect:

- **Arrival and Attire:**
    - Upon entering the hammam, visitors typically change into a provided towel, cloth, or disposable garment (often called a *fouta*). Some hammams also offer the option of wearing swimsuits.
    - You'll be led to the changing area, where you can lock up your belongings in a secure locker.
    - Most hammams separate men and women, but there are a few mixed-gender baths, so be sure to check the establishment's policy beforehand.

- **The Steam Room (Al-Bayt al-Sagheer):**
    - The core of the hammam experience is the steam room. These rooms are typically heated to high temperatures to open the pores and promote deep cleansing.
    - The steam is gentle, helping to relax muscles and prepare the body for the traditional exfoliation process.
    - The atmosphere is dimly lit, with marble floors and walls, and there's often a quiet, tranquil ambiance.
- **Exfoliation and Scrubbing:**
    - After warming up in the steam room, visitors undergo an exfoliating treatment. This is often done by an attendant (sometimes called a *batha* or *scrubber*) using a rough glove called a *kessa*.
    - The scrub is vigorous and thorough, removing dead skin and leaving the body feeling rejuvenated and smooth. You can also ask for a gentle scrub if you have sensitive skin.
    - It's also common for some hammams to offer additional treatments such as body masks made from natural ingredients like clay, olive oil, or honey.
- **Soaping and Rinsing:**
    - After the exfoliation, a thick lather of traditional black soap, made from olive oil and olives, is applied. The soap is rich and moisturizing, and the attendant will massage it into your skin.
    - The soap is followed by a rinse, often using warm water poured from large copper or brass basins.

- **Relaxation and Hydration:**
    - After the cleansing and exfoliation process, you'll move to a cooler room or a lounge area where you can relax, sip on fresh mint tea, and hydrate.
    - It's common to spend at least an hour or more in the hammam, depending on your preferences and the specific treatment package chosen.

Popular Hammams to Visit in Tunis

While many hammams are located in the heart of the Medina, there are also modern and luxury options that offer a blend of traditional treatments with contemporary amenities. Here are a few notable hammams to experience in Tunis:

- **Hammam El-Médina (Medina Hammam):**
    - Located within the bustling Medina of Tunis, Hammam El-Médina is one of the oldest and most iconic bathhouses in the city. It features beautiful mosaic tiles and traditional marble floors, offering a historic atmosphere.
    - The hammam has both male and female sections and offers a range of services, including body scrubs, massages, and traditional steam baths.
- **Hammam Fassis:**
    - Situated in a quieter area of the Medina, Hammam Fassis is known for its serene atmosphere and offers a traditional experience with minimal modern interference.
    - The hammam is smaller, with intimate spaces designed for relaxation and rejuvenation.

- **Dar El Jeld Hammam:**
    - Located in the heart of Tunis, this luxurious hammam combines traditional Tunisian wellness rituals with a modern spa atmosphere. It's one of the more upscale options in the city, offering personalized services like aromatherapy and massage along with traditional scrubbing and soaping.
- **Royal Hammam (Hammam Royal):**
    - Situated in the modern part of Tunis, this luxury hammam is part of a larger hotel and wellness center. It offers high-end services, including private rooms, skin treatments, and access to saunas and Jacuzzis.

Essential Tips for Visiting a Hammam in Tunis

- **Bring Your Own Essentials:** While many hammams provide towels and basic amenities, it's a good idea to bring your own toiletries, such as shampoo, soap, and a loofah. Some visitors also prefer to bring their own slippers and a bathrobe for comfort.
- **Hydrate Before and After:** The heat in the hammam can be intense, so make sure to drink plenty of water before and after your visit to avoid dehydration. You can also enjoy refreshing mint tea after your session, which is a local tradition.
- **Respect the Traditions:** The hammam is a place of relaxation and cleansing, so it's important to maintain a respectful and quiet demeanor. Avoid loud talking or any disruptive behavior to preserve the peaceful environment.

- **Timing Your Visit:** Hammams can get busy, especially on weekends, so if you prefer a quieter experience, try to visit during weekdays or earlier in the day. Some hammams also offer private rooms for a more personalized experience.
- **Treatments and Packages:** Many hammams offer various packages, including facials, massages, and henna tattoos. Be sure to inquire about these when booking to enhance your experience.
- **Avoiding the Rush:** Weekends are usually the busiest times for locals, so visiting during off-peak hours (such as early in the morning) is ideal to get the most out of your experience.

Festivals and Events

Tunis, the vibrant capital of Tunisia, is home to a rich cultural calendar that showcases the country's diverse heritage, art, music, and traditions. Throughout the year, various festivals and events attract travelers from around the world, offering a unique glimpse into Tunisian life. Whether you're a lover of music, film, history, or religious traditions, attending one of these festivals is an unforgettable way to experience the heart of Tunisian culture. Below is an expanded guide to some of the most significant festivals and events that take place in Tunis.

Carthage Film Festival (Journées Cinématographiques de Carthage)

- **When:** November (Biennial)
- **What to Expect:** The Carthage Film Festival is one of the most prestigious film events in the Arab world and Africa, celebrating cinema from the Arab world, Africa, and beyond. Established in 1966, the festival provides a

platform for filmmakers to showcase their work, and it often features screenings of award-winning films, director panels, and discussions on contemporary cinema.
- ○ **Special Highlights:**
    - *Official Competitions:* The festival includes various competitive categories, such as feature films, documentaries, and short films.
    - *Cultural Events:* The festival is accompanied by music performances, art exhibitions, and social gatherings that highlight Tunisia's rich cultural scene.
    - *Red Carpet Events:* Glamorous red-carpet events and award ceremonies offer a chance to see international stars and filmmakers.
- **Essential Tips:**
    - ○ Purchase tickets in advance for popular screenings as they tend to sell out quickly.
    - ○ Many films are shown with English or French subtitles, but some may be in Arabic or French.
    - ○ If you're a film enthusiast, consider attending industry panels and networking events.

International Festival of the Medina (Festival International de la Médina)

- **When:** July and August
- **What to Expect:** Held annually in the historic Medina of Tunis, the International Festival of the Medina is one of the most important cultural festivals in the country. It is a celebration of the arts, offering a program filled with music, theater, dance, and other performances that take

place in the open-air venues within the ancient streets of the Medina. The festival often features both traditional Tunisian art forms and modern performances, making it a perfect representation of Tunisia's evolving cultural landscape.
  - **Special Highlights:**
    - *Traditional Music and Dance:* Enjoy performances of traditional Tunisian music, including *Mouwashah*, *Malouf*, and *Sufi music*, along with vibrant folk dance.
    - *Theater and Opera:* Outdoor performances in the picturesque Medina provide a magical setting for local and international theater troupes and operatic performances.
    - *Art and Handicrafts:* Explore the local arts and crafts, with opportunities to buy traditional Tunisian products like ceramics, carpets, and jewelry from local artisans.
- **Essential Tips:**
  - Most events are free and open to the public, but it's a good idea to arrive early for the best seats, especially for popular performances.
  - Be sure to wear comfortable shoes, as the Medina's cobblestone streets can be uneven.
  - Consider visiting the souks before or after the performances to explore traditional Tunisian crafts.

Tunisian National Day (Fête de la République)

- **When:** July 25
- **What to Expect:** Tunisian National Day celebrates the country's independence and the establishment of the

Republic in 1957. This public holiday marks the abolition of the monarchy and the founding of the modern Tunisian state. The day is marked by grand ceremonies, patriotic parades, and public celebrations, with the President of Tunisia presiding over various official events.
   - **Special Highlights:**
     - *Military Parades:* Watch as soldiers march through Avenue Habib Bourguiba, showcasing Tunisia's military strength.
     - *Cultural Exhibitions:* Museums and galleries may hold special exhibitions focused on the history of Tunisia and its independence.
     - *Public Celebrations:* Expect fireworks, concerts, and street parties, especially in central areas like Tunis' central districts.
- **Essential Tips:**
   - National Day is a public holiday, so expect many shops and businesses to be closed, though restaurants and hotels will likely remain open.
   - Be sure to join in the festivities, but respect local customs, especially during the more solemn aspects of the celebrations.

Ramadan and Eid al-Fitr (End of Ramadan Festival)

- **When:** Varies according to the Islamic lunar calendar (usually around March or April for Ramadan, followed by Eid al-Fitr)
- **What to Expect:** Ramadan is the holy month of fasting for Muslims, and it plays a central role in Tunisian culture. The atmosphere during Ramadan is unique, as the city comes alive after sunset, with people breaking their fast and

engaging in family gatherings. This is followed by the celebration of Eid al-Fitr, the festival that marks the end of Ramadan. The festival is a joyous occasion with prayer services, feasts, and family celebrations.

- **Special Highlights:**
  - *Iftar Feasts:* Join locals as they break their fast at sunset with an elaborate meal that includes traditional dishes such as *brik*, *couscous*, and *baklava*. Many restaurants and hotels offer special iftar menus.
  - *Prayer Services:* Attend special Eid prayers at mosques, including the grand mosques of Tunis like the Zitouna Mosque.
  - *Gifts and Charity:* It's customary to give gifts and charity during Eid, with locals participating in acts of charity to mark the holiday.
- **Essential Tips:**
  - Be mindful of local customs during Ramadan. While tourists are generally not expected to fast, it's respectful to avoid eating, drinking, or smoking in public during daylight hours.
  - Book your accommodations and restaurant reservations well in advance, as many places may be fully booked during this period.
  - During Eid, markets and shops come alive with decorations and special sales.

Mawlid al-Nabi (Prophet Muhammad's Birthday)

- **When:** Varies according to the Islamic lunar calendar (typically October or November)

- **What to Expect:** Mawlid al-Nabi is the celebration of the birth of the Prophet Muhammad, and it is one of the most significant religious holidays in Tunisia. Although not universally celebrated with the same intensity as Eid, it is marked with spiritual gatherings, processions, and public celebrations, particularly in the older parts of Tunis. The day is a time for reflection, charity, and joyous events.
    - **Special Highlights:**
        - *Religious Processions:* Experience processions through the streets, particularly in neighborhoods like the Medina, where large groups of people come together to sing hymns and prayers.
        - *Special Prayers and Sermons:* Attend the prayers at local mosques, where sermons focus on the life of Prophet Muhammad and the teachings of Islam.
        - *Traditional Sweets and Feasts:* Locals prepare and share traditional sweets such as *makroud* and *baklava*, and families come together for large meals.
- **Essential Tips:**
    - While the celebrations are largely religious in nature, visitors can experience the atmosphere by participating in public events or simply observing the processions.
    - Many shops may close during Mawlid al-Nabi, so plan your shopping and dining accordingly.

Festival of Sacred Music of Carthage (Festival de Musique Sacrée de Carthage)

- **When:** April or May
- **What to Expect:** This festival is a unique event dedicated to sacred music from around the world, set against the backdrop of the ancient ruins of Carthage, just outside Tunis. The festival brings together musicians and choirs performing religious and spiritual music from various faiths, including Christianity, Islam, and Judaism, offering a cross-cultural celebration of sacred melodies.
    - **Special Highlights:**
        - *International Performances:* Listen to performances by local and international choirs, classical musicians, and orchestras performing spiritual and religious music.
        - *Historical Venue:* Held in the historic ruins of Carthage, the festival provides a dramatic and evocative setting that enhances the spiritual atmosphere.
        - *Workshops and Discussions:* Attend workshops where performers and scholars discuss the intersections of music, religion, and culture.
- **Essential Tips:**
    - Tickets can be purchased in advance for performances at the Carthage Amphitheater, which offers stunning views of the Mediterranean Sea.
    - Arrive early to find seating, as the amphitheater fills quickly, especially for popular events.

Religious Sites and Traditions in Tunis

Tunis, the capital of Tunisia, is not only a center for political and cultural life but also a hub for the country's rich religious traditions. The city's history is deeply intertwined with Islam, though the influence of Christianity and Judaism has also left its mark. Religious sites, ranging from ancient mosques to tranquil cemeteries and churches, offer visitors the opportunity to delve into Tunisia's spiritual heritage. The following guide explores the most significant religious sites and traditions in Tunis, providing travelers with an understanding of the sacred practices and spaces that shape the identity of this North African city.

The Great Mosque of Zitouna

- **Overview:** One of the oldest and most revered religious structures in Tunisia, the **Great Mosque of Zitouna** (Jami' al-Zaytuna), is a symbol of Islamic heritage and a focal point of religious life in Tunis. Established in the 8th century, the mosque has long been an important center for education, scholarship, and religious practice.
    - **What to Expect:**
        - The mosque's architecture blends Arab, Andalusian, and Byzantine influences, featuring a large central courtyard, beautiful arches, and a majestic minaret. The interior is just as captivating, with intricate mosaics, cedar wood carvings, and Islamic calligraphy adorning the walls.
        - Zitouna has historically been a center of Islamic learning, and its influence on Tunisia's spiritual and intellectual life cannot be overstated.
        - The mosque is also home to a large library, which holds important religious texts and manuscripts.

- **Visiting Tips:**
  - **Dress Modestly:** As a place of worship, visitors should dress conservatively and respectfully.
  - **Prayer Times:** The mosque is an active place of worship, so visitors should avoid visiting during prayer times.
  - **Location:** Situated in the heart of the Medina of Tunis, the mosque is easily accessible, and a visit to the nearby souks and markets adds to the overall experience.

The Mosque of Al-Djem

- **Overview:** Located just outside of Tunis, in the town of **El Djem**, the **Grand Mosque of Al-Djem** is one of Tunisia's most impressive historical and architectural landmarks. Though it is located in a more rural setting, its size and historical significance make it a worthy visit.
  - **What to Expect:**
    - Originally built in the 9th century, the mosque combines traditional Islamic design with influences from Roman architecture. The site is famous for its large prayer hall and an ancient Roman amphitheater nearby, showing the blending of Tunisia's Christian, Roman, and Islamic past.
    - The mosque is an important site for religious and community gatherings, offering visitors a deeper understanding of Tunisia's religious practices.
- **Visiting Tips:**

- **Timing:** Visit during the cooler hours of the day, as it can get quite hot in the summer months.
- **Access to Ruins:** The nearby ruins and the Roman amphitheater are often included in guided tours, providing insight into the historical context of the region.

The Cathedral of St. Vincent de Paul

- **Overview:** Although Islam dominates the religious landscape of Tunisia, the **Cathedral of St. Vincent de Paul**, located in central Tunis, stands as a testament to the country's rich Christian heritage. Built in the early 20th century during the French colonial period, the cathedral's neo-Gothic design and towering spires are a striking feature of the city's skyline.
  - **What to Expect:**
    - The cathedral is dedicated to St. Vincent de Paul, the patron saint of charity, and it is one of the few Catholic churches in the country that still holds regular services. The interior of the church is beautifully adorned with stained glass windows, intricate mosaics, and sculptures.
    - Although the majority of the Christian population has left Tunisia, the cathedral still serves as an important site for the small Christian community in Tunis, and it remains open to visitors who are interested in the country's Christian history.
- **Visiting Tips:**

- o **Respecting Worship Services:** Visitors should be mindful of the services and events being held in the cathedral.
- o **Open Hours:** The cathedral is open to tourists most days, though hours can vary, so it's advisable to check in advance.

The Jewish Quarter and El Ghriba Synagogue

- **Overview:** Tunisia has a long history of Jewish presence, with communities living on the island of Djerba and in parts of Tunis for centuries. The **El Ghriba Synagogue** is one of the oldest synagogues in North Africa and a significant Jewish pilgrimage site. Though located in the town of Hara, on the island of Djerba, many visitors to Tunis include it as part of a cultural exploration of Tunisia's Jewish heritage.
  - o **What to Expect:**
    - The synagogue is famous for its distinctive architecture, with a serene courtyard and the presence of thousands of colorful votive offerings left by pilgrims. The El Ghriba Synagogue is particularly notable for its annual pilgrimage, which draws Jews from across the world.
    - Tunis itself is home to a vibrant Jewish community, with the old **Jewish Quarter** in the Medina offering a fascinating glimpse into the everyday life of the Tunisian Jewish community. The area is dotted with Jewish-owned businesses, kosher restaurants, and beautifully adorned Jewish houses.

- **Visiting Tips:**
  - **Respectful Exploration:** The synagogue is still an active place of worship, so visitors should be respectful during religious observances.
  - **Accessibility:** Djerba is approximately 5 hours by road from Tunis, so a visit to the island requires a full-day trip.

Sidi Mahrez Mosque

- **Overview:** Located in the Medina of Tunis, the **Sidi Mahrez Mosque** is a beautiful example of traditional Tunisian mosque architecture. Named after a revered local saint, Sidi Mahrez, this mosque is less visited by tourists than the Great Mosque of Zitouna, but it offers a quiet place to reflect on Tunisian religious life.
  - **What to Expect:**
    - The mosque features ornate stucco work, finely carved wood doors, and an impressive minaret that towers above the surrounding buildings. The interior is known for its simplicity, which contrasts with the more elaborate decorations found in other mosques.
    - Sidi Mahrez Mosque plays an important role in the spiritual life of the people of Tunis, particularly in the old Medina.
- **Visiting Tips:**
  - **Access:** The mosque is open to visitors outside of prayer times, though dress code and respectful behavior are required.

- o **Local Community:** Since the mosque is frequently visited by locals, it is a great spot to observe Tunisian religious practices and the daily rhythm of the Medina.

Sufi Shrines and Rituals

- **Overview:** Sufism, the mystical branch of Islam, has a long and rich history in Tunisia, and the city of Tunis is home to several important Sufi shrines. These shrines are places of worship and spiritual reflection, where Sufi orders engage in devotional practices such as dhikr (remembrance of God) and the famous whirling dances.
  - o **What to Expect:**
    - Sufi shrines in Tunis, such as the **Sidi El Bechir** and **Sidi Bou Saïd**, offer travelers a chance to experience the peaceful and meditative side of Islam. These shrines often have a tranquil atmosphere, surrounded by lush gardens and peaceful courtyards.
    - **Sufi Music and Dance:** In addition to the religious ceremonies, Sufi music and the whirling dervishes' dance are sometimes performed at these shrines, providing a unique experience of Islamic mysticism.
- **Visiting Tips:**
  - o **Participation:** Visitors are often welcome to attend Sufi rituals, though it's important to be respectful of the sacred nature of the ceremonies.
  - o **Time:** Whirling dervish ceremonies typically occur in the evening, so planning ahead is essential.

Tunisian Ramadan Traditions

- **Overview:** Ramadan is an important religious observance for Muslims around the world, and Tunisia is no exception. During this holy month, the city of Tunis comes alive with special traditions, from nightly feasts to religious rituals.
  - **What to Expect:**
    - The **iftar** meal, breaking the fast at sunset, is a significant cultural experience in Tunis. Travelers can join in the local tradition by visiting restaurants or family homes to enjoy traditional dishes like **brik**, **harira soup**, and **dates**.
    - **Taraweeh Prayers:** Throughout Ramadan, the mosques in Tunis hold special prayers called **taraweeh**, where the entire Quran is recited. Visitors are encouraged to experience these prayers if they are in the city during the holy month.
- **Visiting Tips:**
  - **Respecting the Fast:** During Ramadan, travelers should be mindful of local customs, such as refraining from eating or drinking in public during daylight hours.
  - **Evening Exploration:** The atmosphere in Tunis changes significantly after sunset, with the streets coming alive as people break their fast and engage in communal gatherings.

Cultural experiences in Tunis are diverse, enriching, and accessible, offering travelers the opportunity to immerse themselves in the country's fascinating heritage. Whether you're indulging in local cuisine, relaxing in a traditional hammam, exploring lively souks, or attending a festival, Tunis will captivate your senses and leave you with lasting memories of its unique blend of ancient traditions and modern charm.

PRACTICAL INFORMATION

Internet and Connectivity

Staying connected while in Tunis is relatively easy, with several options available for accessing the internet. Many hotels, cafes, and restaurants offer free Wi-Fi, though speeds may vary depending on the location. If you're staying for a longer period or need reliable internet access, consider purchasing a local SIM card. Major Tunisian mobile operators like *Tunisie Telecom*, *Orange Tunisia*, and *Ooredoo* offer prepaid SIM cards with affordable data plans. These can be purchased at the airport, in stores, or from kiosks around the city. Ensure your phone is unlocked to use local SIM cards.

For those needing higher speeds or a secure connection, co-working spaces and cafes often cater to digital nomads and provide excellent Wi-Fi.

Health and Safety

Tunis is generally a safe city for travelers, but like in any major urban area, it's essential to take standard precautions. Always keep an eye on your belongings, especially in crowded areas like souks, public transportation, and tourist attractions.

Healthcare Facilities

Tunis has good healthcare facilities, with both public and private hospitals. Private clinics offer high-quality care and are often preferred by travelers. Pharmacies are also widely available, and many carry over-the-counter medications, though some prescription drugs may be difficult to find. It's advisable to carry any specific medications you might need.

If you require emergency medical attention, the phone number to call for an ambulance is *190*. Travelers are encouraged to have travel insurance that covers medical care in case of accidents or illnesses.

Health Precautions

- **Water**: While tap water in Tunis is generally considered safe for consumption, some travelers prefer to drink bottled water, which is widely available.
- **Vaccinations**: There are no mandatory vaccinations for travelers to Tunisia, but it's recommended to be up-to-date on routine vaccinations. Additionally, consider vaccinations for hepatitis A, hepatitis B, and typhoid, especially if you plan to visit rural areas.
- **Sun Protection**: The sun in Tunis can be intense, especially in summer, so bring sunscreen, a hat, and sunglasses to protect yourself from sunburn.

Money Matters

The local currency in Tunisia is the *Tunisian Dinar* (TND). Currency exchange is available at the airport, banks, exchange offices, and many hotels. However, exchange rates might not be as favorable at hotels, so it's better to use official exchange offices or ATMs.

Credit cards are widely accepted at major hotels, shopping malls, and restaurants, though smaller establishments may prefer cash.

International credit cards like Visa and MasterCard are the most commonly accepted. ATMs are also readily available throughout the city, and you can withdraw local currency using your foreign debit or credit card.

Tipping

Tipping is common in Tunisia and generally appreciated. While not mandatory, leaving a tip of about 10-15% at restaurants is customary if service is not included in the bill. For hotel staff, taxis, and guides, small tips for good service are also expected.

Local Language

The official language of Tunisia is *Arabic*, specifically Tunisian Arabic (Derja), which is widely spoken. French is also commonly used in business, government, and education, and many people in the tourism industry speak some level of English. While many locals can understand basic English, it's helpful to learn a few key Arabic phrases or French expressions to navigate daily interactions more smoothly.

Common Phrases:

- *As-salāmu 'alaykum* – Hello (Peace be upon you)
- *Shukran* – Thank you
- *Min faḍlik* – Please
- *Kam al-thaman?* – How much is this?
- *Ayna al-matār?* – Where is the airport?

Emergency and Useful Phone Numbers

In case of an emergency, it's essential to have quick access to the relevant phone numbers:

- **Emergency Ambulance**: 190
- **Police**: 197
- **Fire Department**: 198
- **Tourism Police**: 1717
- **Road Assistance**: 1811
- **General Emergency Services**: 112 (this is the European emergency number and is functional in Tunisia)

If you need to contact your embassy or consulate, you can find their contact information online or through your local embassy in Tunis.

Local Laws

As a visitor in Tunisia, it's crucial to respect local laws and customs to avoid any issues during your stay:

1. **Alcohol**: Alcohol is legal in Tunisia and available in bars, restaurants, and supermarkets, though it is considered a private matter and is not consumed openly in public places like streets. Public drunkenness is frowned upon.
2. **Dress Code**: Tunisia is a predominantly Muslim country, and it's respectful to dress modestly, especially in religious or rural areas. In tourist hubs like the beach or resort areas, casual clothing is acceptable, but avoid wearing revealing clothing in public places outside of these areas.
3. **Photography**: Be cautious when taking photos, particularly in government buildings, military zones, and near people

without their permission. Avoid taking photos of military personnel or police officers.
4. **Drugs**: The possession or use of illegal drugs is strictly prohibited, and penalties can be severe. Even small amounts of illicit substances can result in heavy fines or imprisonment.
5. **Same-Sex Relationships**: Homosexuality is illegal in Tunisia, and same-sex acts are punishable by law. While same-sex relationships are not openly discussed, the country has a growing tolerance for LGBTQ+ tourists, though discretion is advised.

Useful Websites and Resources

Online Maps and Navigation Apps

- Make use of online maps like Google Maps or Maps.me to navigate the Tunis effortlessly. Be sure to download offline maps for regions with limited internet access, allowing you to explore the city's streets, attractions, and neighborhoods with ease.

Tour Operator Websites

- Research and book tours through reputable tour operators. Websites like **GetYourGuide, Viator, or local operators' official sites** offer various excursions, ensuring a well-organized and enjoyable exploration of Tunis attractions.

Weather Updates

- Stay informed about Tunis weather conditions through reliable weather websites or apps like AccuWeather. This ensures you pack appropriately and plan outdoor activities on days with favorable weather.

Language Learning Resources

To facilitate communication and enhance your cultural immersion, consider language learning resources

- **Duolingo** (www.duolingo.com): A popular language-learning app.
- **Google Translate**: Google Translate can be incredibly helpful for interacting with locals who might not speak English. This free translation app enables real-time translation of both text and speech. It's an excellent tool for engaging with residents and navigating the city. Additionally, you can use the app to photograph signs or menus and get instant translations. For offline access, download the **Arabic** language pack to facilitate easier communication with locals.

However, keep in mind that machine translations like Google Translate are not always perfect, and there may be nuances in language or culture that the app may not fully capture.

Hotel/Accommodation Booking Platforms

- Use reputable booking platforms such as **Booking.com**, **Airbnb**, or **Expedia** to secure accommodation. Read reviews, compare prices, and choose lodgings that align with your preferences and budget.

TripAdvisor (tripadvisor.com)

- Plan and book accommodations, restaurants, and activities based on traveler reviews.
- Access travel forums for advice and tips from experienced travelers.

Hotel or Accommodation Front Desk:

- Your hotel or accommodation's front desk can provide assistance with various inquiries, including arranging transportation, booking tours or excursions, and addressing any concerns during your stay.

By embracing the local customs and preparing for potential challenges, you'll be able to fully immerse yourself in the unique charm and cultural richness that Tunis has to offer. Safe travels and enjoy your adventure!

18 MUST-DO ACTIVITIES FOR A MEMORABLE EXPERIENCE IN TUNIS

Tunis, with its stunning landscapes, rich history, and vibrant culture, offers an array of activities that promise an unforgettable experience. Here's 18 to-do list to ensure you make the most of your visit to this beautiful destination.

1. **Wander Through the Medina of Tunis**

   - Explore the UNESCO-listed Medina, with its narrow alleys, vibrant souks, and historic buildings. Don't miss the *Zitouna Mosque* and the bustling *Place de la Kasbah*.

2. **Visit the Bardo National Museum**

   - Discover Tunisia's rich history at one of the most important museums in the country, home to an impressive collection of Roman mosaics and ancient artifacts.

3. **Tour the Ancient Ruins of Carthage**

   - Step back in time and explore the ruins of this once-powerful city, with highlights including the *Antonine Baths*, *Carthage National Museum*, and *Carthage's Roman Theater*.

4. **Relax in the Picturesque Sidi Bou Said**

   - Experience the iconic blue-and-white village of Sidi Bou Said, known for its stunning views, cobblestone streets, and charming cafes overlooking the Mediterranean.

5. **Visit the Roman Amphitheater in El Jem**

    - Take a day trip to El Jem and marvel at the well-preserved Roman amphitheater, one of the largest in the world, once hosting gladiator battles and chariot races.

6. **Explore the Ruins of Dougga**

    - Venture into the countryside to visit Dougga, an ancient Roman town that boasts stunning ruins like the *Capitol Temple* and *Roman Theater* amidst scenic landscapes.

7. **Stroll Through the Souks of Tunis**

    - Dive into Tunisian culture at the lively souks where you can shop for handcrafted goods, spices, textiles, and jewelry, and haggle for the best prices.

8. **Enjoy Tunisian Cuisine at a Traditional Restaurant**

    - Savor classic dishes like *couscous*, *brik* (fried pastry), *mechoui* (roast lamb), and *harissa* (spicy paste) at local eateries.

9. **Spend a Day at the Beach in La Marsa**

    - Escape the city heat with a relaxing day at La Marsa's beautiful beaches, offering sandy shores and crystal-clear waters perfect for swimming and sunbathing.

10. **Visit the Mosque of Youssef Dey**

- Admire the stunning architecture and intricate design of this historical mosque, located in the heart of the Medina, offering a quiet retreat from the bustling streets.

11. Take a Boat Ride to the Tunisian Islands

- Head to the *Kerkennah Islands* or *Djerba* for a peaceful boat ride and enjoy their unspoiled beaches, traditional fishing villages, and local culture.

12. Discover the Richness of the Tunisian Jewelry Tradition

- Visit local markets and jewelry workshops where you can watch artisans craft stunning silver and gold jewelry, often with intricate designs influenced by Berber and Arab traditions.

13. Walk Along the Avenue Habib Bourguiba

- Enjoy a leisurely walk down this tree-lined boulevard, the heart of modern Tunis, where you'll find cafes, luxury shops, and beautiful colonial-era buildings.

14. Relax in the Public Gardens of Belvedere

- Escape the city's hustle and bustle with a visit to the Belvedere Park, offering lush greenery, lake views, and a chance to unwind amidst nature.

15. Explore the El Abidine Palace

- Visit this grand palace, once the residence of the ruling family, and admire its beautiful architecture, including intricate tile work, decorative fountains, and landscaped gardens.

16. Watch a Traditional Tunisian Music Performance

- Attend a traditional music performance such as *Malouf*, a genre of classical Tunisian music, or explore the vibrant local jazz scene at one of the city's music venues.

17. Take a Guided Tour of the Medina's Historic Landmarks

- Enhance your experience with a knowledgeable guide who can share fascinating insights about the historic mosques, madrasas, and landmarks scattered throughout the Medina.

18. Shop for Tunisian Carpets and Textiles

- Don't leave Tunis without visiting the artisan carpet workshops or markets. These handwoven treasures come in beautiful designs and colors, reflecting Tunisia's rich textile tradition.

SUGGESTED ITINERARY FOR EXPLORING TUNIS

Tunis is a perfect destination for travelers seeking a mix of relaxation and adventure. This week-long itinerary will guide you through her highlights, offering a balanced blend of culture, nature, and leisure activities.

Day 1: Arrival and Orientation in Tunis
- **Morning**: Arrive at Tunis-Carthage International Airport. Transfer to your hotel and settle in. Choose accommodation near the Medina or in a modern neighborhood like Lac or Berges du Lac for convenience.
- **Afternoon**: Head to the Medina of Tunis, a vibrant labyrinth of narrow streets and bustling souks. Visit landmarks like the Zitouna Mosque, the heart of the Medina, and explore artisanal shops offering ceramics, jewelry, and traditional clothing.
- **Evening**: Dine at a local restaurant such as Dar El Jeld, known for its authentic Tunisian cuisine, and enjoy dishes like tagine or couscous paired with mint tea.

Day 2: Explore Carthage and Sidi Bou Said
- **Morning**: Travel to Carthage, an ancient Phoenician city rich in history. Explore iconic ruins, including the Antonine Baths, Carthage Amphitheater, and Byrsa Hill, offering panoramic views.
- **Afternoon**: Continue to Sidi Bou Said, a stunning village known for its blue-and-white architecture. Stroll through cobblestone streets, browse boutique shops, and admire the

sea views from Dar El Annabi, a cultural museum housed in a traditional home.
- **Evening**: Enjoy a leisurely dinner at Le Pirate or another seaside restaurant with fresh seafood specialties before heading back to Tunis.

Day 3: Museums and Cultural Heritage
- **Morning**: Visit the Bardo Museum, housed in a former palace. Marvel at its vast collection of Roman mosaics, Islamic art, and historical artifacts that span centuries of Tunisian culture.
- **Afternoon**: Explore Belvédère Park, a serene escape in the city. Wander through its landscaped gardens and visit the **Tunis Zoo** for a family-friendly activity.
- **Evening**: Unwind with dinner at Chez Slah, a popular restaurant known for its blend of traditional and modern Tunisian dishes.

Day 4: Day Trip to Dougga
- **Full Day**: Embark on a guided tour to Dougga, a UNESCO World Heritage Site located about two hours from Tunis. Known as the "Rome of North Africa," Dougga is home to well-preserved Roman ruins, including the Capitol, Theater, and Temple of Saturn. Learn about the city's history as you wander through its ancient streets.
- **Evening**: Return to Tunis and enjoy a quiet evening reflecting on the day's discoveries. Opt for a light dinner or relax with a cup of traditional herbal tea.

Day 5: Beach and Relaxation in La Marsa

- **Morning**: Head to La Marsa, a chic coastal area perfect for relaxation. Spend time on its sandy beaches or take a leisurely stroll along the promenade while enjoying the sea breeze.
- **Afternoon**: Indulge in lunch at a beachfront café like Saf-Saf, famous for its delicious couscous and traditional ambiance. Afterward, visit El Abidine Mosque, known for its modern yet elegant design.
- **Evening**: Dine at a high-end restaurant in La Marsa, savoring fresh fish or traditional dishes with a modern twist.

Day 6: Market Day and Culinary Delights

- **Morning**: Immerse yourself in local life by visiting the Marché Central de Tunis, the central market bustling with vendors selling fresh produce, spices, and traditional ingredients. Engage with locals and learn about Tunisian staples.
- **Afternoon**: Take part in a Tunisian cooking class hosted by a local chef. Learn to prepare signature dishes like harissa, brik (a crispy pastry filled with egg and tuna), and tagine.
- **Evening**: Feast on the dishes you prepared during the class and share stories with fellow participants.

Day 7: Final Exploration and Departure

- **Morning**: Revisit the Medina to pick up last-minute souvenirs such as handwoven carpets, pottery, or olive oil. Alternatively, explore modern shopping areas like Berges du Lac for a different vibe.

- **Afternoon**: Relax at a nearby café, sipping Turkish coffee or refreshing lemonade while soaking in the city's atmosphere. Return to your hotel to prepare for your departure.
- **Evening**: Transfer to Tunis-Carthage International Airport for your flight home, leaving with lasting memories of Tunisia's vibrant culture and history.

Feel free to adjust the itinerary based on your interests and preferences. Tunis offers a diverse range of experiences, from cultural immersion to breathtaking natural wonders.

CONCLUSION

Tunis is a city where history, culture, and modernity come together in a vibrant and unforgettable experience. From the ancient ruins of Carthage to the lively souks of the Medina, every corner of this city tells a story. Whether you're wandering the blue-and-white streets of Sidi Bou Said, marveling at the treasures of the Bardo Museum, or savoring the flavors of Tunisian cuisine, there's something here for every traveler.

As you explore its diverse landscapes and rich heritage, Tunis will captivate you with its warmth and charm. This travel guide has provided you with the tools to uncover the best of what the city has to offer. Wherever your journey takes you, may Tunis leave you with memories to cherish and a deeper appreciation for this remarkable destination.

As you embark on your travels, remember the practical tips provided in this guide. Being aware of the local customs, transportation options, and essential services will help ensure a smooth and enjoyable trip. Engaging with the locals and embracing their way of life will enrich your experience and create lasting memories.

We encourage you to embrace the spirit of exploration, immerse yourself in the local culture, and savor every moment of your time in Tunis.

As you plan your trip to Tunis, keep in mind that this guide is just the beginning. Tunis is a dynamic and ever-changing place, with new attractions and experiences popping up all the time. So don't be afraid to explore beyond the pages of this guidebook and discover the place for yourself.

We hope this guide has provided you with the inspiration and information you need to plan fun activities in Tunis. Whether you're visiting for the first time or returning for a repeat visit, we know you will fall in love with this beautiful destination and all that it has to offer.

ON A FINAL NOTE

The information presented in this travel guide is intended for general informational purposes, and considerable effort has been exerted to ensure the accuracy of the information. Readers are urged to exercise their discretion and take responsibility for their own travel decisions and activities when implementing the suggestions and recommendations found in this guide. Please be aware that details such as prices, operational hours, and other specifics are subject to change without prior notice. It is advisable to verify this information with relevant authorities, businesses, or organizations before finalizing any travel plans or reservations.

It is essential to clarify that the mention of particular products, services, businesses, or organizations in this guide does not imply an endorsement by the author. Readers are strongly encouraged to observe necessary precautions and adhere to local laws, regulations, and customs. The author and publisher of this travel guide disclaim any responsibility for inaccuracies or omissions and disclaim liability for any potential damages or losses resulting from the application of the information provided herein.

Thank you for choosing this guide, until we meet again on another adventure.

PEN NOTES

Made in the USA
Middletown, DE
22 February 2025

71654578R00151